A CENTENNIAL CELEBRATION

100 Years
IN PICTURES

FEATURING NEW ESSAYS BY
CHARLES ELLIOTT

Outdoor Life
100 Years in Pictures

Essays by Charles Elliott, *Outdoor Life* Contributing Editor
Introduction by Todd W. Smith, *Outdoor Life* Editor-in-Chief

President: Iain Macfarlane
Group Director, Book Development: Zoe Graul
Creative Director: Lisa Rosenthal
Senior Managing Editor: Elaine Perry

Executive Editor, Outdoor Group: Don Oster
Project Leader and Contributing Writer: David R. Maas
Managing Editor: Denise Bornhausen
Associate Creative Director: Brad Springer
Photographers: Chuck Nields and Greg Wallace
Copy Editor: Janice Cauley
Desktop Publishing Specialists: Eileen Bovard and Laurie Kristensen
Publishing Production Manager: Kim Gerber

Special thanks to: Jason E. Klein, President, *Outdoor Life*; Camille Cozzone Rankin, Bob Brown,
Ed Scheff and the staff of *Outdoor Life* magazine; Kevin Adams; Guy Chambers; John Fletcher;
Tom Heck; Highwood Book Shop; Iowa State University Library; Thomas McKinnon; the
photo studio staff of Cowles Creative Publishing; Pete Press; Southdale Hennepin (Co. MN)
Area Library; Vin T. Sparano; Tracy Stanley; David Tieszen; and the University of Minnesota
Entomology, Fisheries and Wildlife Library

Printed on American Paper by: R. R. Donnelley & Sons Co.
02 01 00 99 98 / 5 4 3 2 1

The Library of Congress Cataloging-in-Publication Data
Outdoor life : 100 years in pictures / featuring new essays by Charles Elliott.
           p. cm.
        "A centennial celebration."
      ISBN 0-86573-075-X (hardcover)
      1. Hunting--West (U.S.)--Pictorial works. 2. Fishing--West (U.S.)--Pictorial works.
   3. Outdoor life--West (U.S.)--Pictorial works. I. Elliott, Charles Newton, 1906-   .
   II. Outdoor life (Denver, Colo.)
   SK45.087 1998
   799.2'022'2--dc21   97-49710

Table of Contents

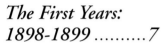

Introduction

"Few inventions have revolutionized the art of illustrating to a greater extent than the invention of the hand camera; in conjunction with photoengraving it did for art what the printing press and movable type did for typography."

—Hugo Erichsen, M.D., Outdoor Life, January 1901

Magazines have always presented an interesting challenge to editors. How do you bring life and movement to the flat plane of a printed page? There are no microchips or sound bites to enhance the words; no special effects or techno-wizardy to bring the printed type to life. In the end, an editor's only tools are words and pictures.

Great magazines begin with great writing. In this regard, *Outdoor Life* has been a showcase for great outdoor authors since its inception. Founding editor J.A. McGuire knew a good story when he saw one. He also understood the delicate balance between words and pictures and how, in the right proportions, pictures can help draw in the reader and take an otherwise good story to new heights.

This is why the Computer Age presents such a paradox. The goal today is to be "interactive"—a term stolen from videography—inviting the user to "play along" with what's happening on the screen. Welcome to the 21st century. And yet, I'm convinced that my predecessors at *Outdoor Life* had the interactive concept figured out a long time ago. They didn't do it with high-tech sleight of hand. They invited the reader to engage in a far more primitive form of interaction called the "imagination." The pictures merely reinforced the power of the writing to draw the reader in further.

What follows is a perfect example of how words combined with pictures can be used to tell an even more compelling story than either would have done alone. The words come courtesy of Charles Elliott, who's 91 years old and the holder of the longest continuous masthead position at *Outdoor Life* (nearly 50 years).

In Charlie's inimitable style, you'll get a firsthand account of exactly how certain stories and events shaped the pages of *Outdoor Life*. How different editors molded the publication. How the magazine dealt with world wars, game-management crises, advances in technology and so much more. It's superb writing and a tribute to a man who has given his entire life to conservation and to sharing his love of the outdoors with others.

Charlie's essays serve as the perfect backdrop to highlight some of the wonderful photographs, drawings and covers that have graced *Outdoor Life* these past 100 years. In paging through, it's easy to see how J.A. McGuire, and the editors who followed him, used pictures to extend the scope of the publication. Photos were used both as instructional tools and as a way to bring the vitality and movement of the great outdoors to the magazine's pages. The power of photography was also harnessed to drive home political points and to bolster the magazine's editorial stance on sensitive issues.

It was the powerful images of sagging meatpoles and market hunters' boats jammed to the gunwales with ducks that provided the impetus for the enactment of conservation legislation in this country. And it was the images of Isle Royal, the Everglades, giant sequoias and Yellowstone Falls that helped sway Congress to protect these areas within a National Parks system.

Of equal power and importance were the many paintings used as cover images for *Outdoor Life* over the years. They cover a wide variety of styles, from impressionistic views of the Wild West to human-interest portrayals that could very well have served as cover art for *The Saturday Evening Post*.

At the heart of all of these images is the celebration of the American spirit of adventure and the simple joy of being out in nature that every outdoorsman can appreciate.

It is fitting that in celebrating *Outdoor Life's* 100th anniversary this book should combine the talents of the magazine's most senior editor and many of the most famous photos and art pieces that have brought the thrill of the outdoors to life for millions of readers. I know that J.A. McGuire would be as impressed and proud of this heritage as I am.

Todd W. Smith

Todd W. Smith, Editor-in-Chief
November 15, 1997
Rye, New York

Vol. I.   **JANUARY, 1898.**   **No. I.**

Table of Contents

DEPARTMENTS

PHOTOGRAPHY   TRAP AND TARGET
IN THE GAME FIELD   EDITORIAL
BY MAIL   CYCLING

10c a Copy   **$1.00 a Year**

The First Years 1898-1899

DURING OUR NATION'S PRIMITIVE YEARS, AMERICA HAD STRUGGLED TO DRIVE BACK THE WILDERNESS, DECLARED ITSELF AN INDEPENDENT NATION AND FOUGHT A WAR TO PROVE IT, AND THEN OVERHARVESTED THE WEALTH THAT CAME WITH FREEDOM.

History was written in those years before and after we became a nation, and much of it involved the wealth of the vast natural resources we found in this virgin New World. It was so very bountiful that we squandered it, believing that it would last forever.

The first game provision after Colonial days was passed in Pennsylvania in 1776. It was a constitutional directive that state residents "shall have liberty to fowl and hunt in seasonable times on lands they hold, and all other lands therein not enclosed."

In 1777, North Carolina established regulations to prohibit hunting deer at night with a light, and the next year New Hampshire passed a law protecting whitetail deer from January 1 to August 1, with two persons selected in each town to enforce this provision. This appears to be the first "game warden" system in America. From this date the other states followed the trend with laws for closed seasons and limits.

In 1832, the federal government made its first move in game conservation by creating an act to allow the taking of game animals in Indian Territory only by Indians, except in emergencies. Not until 1871 did Congress introduce a bill to protect the buffalo and pass the first federal game law, setting seasons and limits on a number of game species and restrictions on wildlife classified as non-game.

When *Outdoor Life* made its appearance in 1898, most of the states had set up regulations for seasons and limits for the taking of wild creatures, and that year the first Lacey Act was introduced to Congress for the protection of song birds. *Outdoor Life* quickly became the voice of the sportsman. From the beginning, it was devoted to the pleasures of hunting and fishing and to the perpetuation of those pleasures by condemning lawlessness and greediness. The stories were about sportsmen and sportsmanship and recommended tactics for successful results. Editorially and otherwise, *Outdoor Life* deplored those practices that had been responsible for our vanishing game supply.

By the year 1898, the Oklahoma homestead rush was over and hostilities between the white man and red man were now a bitter bit of history. *Outdoor Life* came into existence two years before the turn of the century. It was fathered by John A. McGuire and inked its first words in Denver, Colorado, in 1898.

John A. McGuire was the outdoorsman of the hour. Born in Iowa, he moved at age 13 to Denver, where he became more deeply involved in outdoor activities. He was dedicated to the bicycle as his means of transportation. At age 18 he was cycling editor for *Sports Afield* and five years later created his first magazine, *Cycling West.* This he sold when he started *Outdoor Life,* but he carried over his cycling interests, and a sizeable portion of his space in the new magazine was devoted to cycling.

Early in *Outdoor Life's* youth, McGuire dedicated his publication strictly to true experiences. This may have been the result of reader reaction to the first issue, in which the lead story was pure fiction.

The remainder of this Number One issue, however, was devoted to hunting and fishing stories, with six pages dedicated to skeet and trap shooting and thirteen pages to cycling.

The avowed statement in this first issue was the foundation for future issues: "We propose to represent and reflect the interest of every devotee of *Outdoor Life* and its attendant sports recreation, as well as those tradesmen who cater to and supply their demands."

Breakfast in the Rockies —
"This is a familiar scene to all who have camped in the rockies. On the left, just under the black streak of rock on the top of the ridge, can be seen the beginning of what one day was a snow slide."

1898

A Mighty Spread —

"My first ball, caught him in the short ribs on the right side and stopped at the skin in front of the left shoulder; he stopped and swung around broadside. I sent another clean through him. He headed off again and I pitched another one into him. He again stopped broadside and coughed hard and when his great sides would heave I saw the blood spout from the wounds."

From "A Moose Hunt in Alaska," by Dall DeWeese

AUGUST, 1898.

Outdoor life

An Illustrated Monthly Magazine of Recreation *Published by* THE OUTDOOR LIFE PUBLISHING CO. Denver Colorado *Yearly Subscrip-* •*tion $1.00* Single Copies 10 Cents

"A group of Ute Indians, visitors at Festival of Mountain and Plain, Denver, Oct. 5-6-7, 1897."

Quite a Change —
From the Outdoor Life *department, "Cycling."*

"Canyon of the grand river, near Glenwood Springs, showing the mirror."
From "Supreme Moments at Angling," by Lewis B. France

1899

MARCH, 1899.

Outdoor Life

An Illustrated Monthly Magazine of Recreation *Published by* THE OUTDOOR LIFE PUBLISHING CO. Denver Colorado *Yearly Subscription* $1.00 Single Copies 10 Cents

A Colorado Sportman's Resort —

"Mr. Snyder's display of rare game animal heads at the Snyder House at Walden, North Park, Colorado. The hostelry is located in the heart of the game country and is presided over by a gentleman who is himself a hale and hearty personage well met."

"Filled his hat with water and then raised it to his lips."
From "Two Shots," by A. Tenderfoot

"As fine a specimen as you often come across."
Mr. Spaulding with his large buck, killed at 250 yards with a 30-40.
From "A Hunt in Northwest Colorado," by W.T. Cornwall

DENVER AND RIO GRANDE RAILROAD

"SCENIC LINE OF THE WORLD" DOUBLE DAILY TRAIN SERVICE FAST TIME AND BEST ACCOMMODATIONS FOR ALL POINTS IN COLORADO UTAH AND THE PACIFIC COAST

FORM D. E.T. JEFFERY PRES'T & GEN'L MANAGER A.S. HUGHES TRAFFIC MANAGER S.K. HOOPER G.P & T.A. DENVER

A Catch of Heavyweights —

"John E. Osborne of Wyoming displays his twelve rainbow trout, weighing a total of fifty-two pounds."

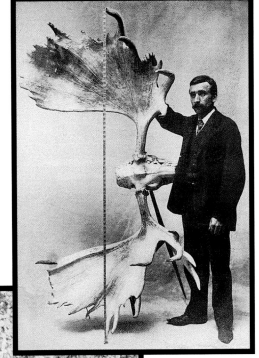

The Monarch of Them All —

"Largest moose antlers on record – spread 78½ inches, with forty-three prongs. Owned by W.F. Sheard, Tacoma, Wash."

Chief Isaac —

Brought from the Flathead Reservation in northwest Montana as a participant in the Indian Carnival of Anaconda, Montana.

From "The Flathead Indians," by D.C. Walker

A Desperate Shot

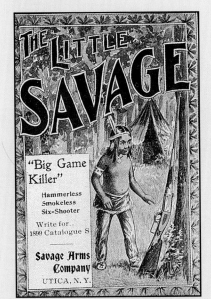

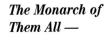

OUTDOOR LIFE

April 1908

LIFE

Price 15¢

GREGG

Best Of The 1900s

IN THESE MODERN TIMES, WITH FASTER-THAN-SOUND AIRCRAFT AND THE WIZARDRY OF TELECOMMUNICATION AND COMPUTERS, IT IS DIFFICULT TO BELIEVE WHAT AN ENTIRELY DIFFERENT WORLD AMERICANS LIVED IN ONE HUNDRED YEARS AGO.

The telephone was a quarter of a century old but was struggling painfully through its early stages of growth. Electric lights had been in existence for two decades only and were more of a novelty than a common utility. Almost all of our nation's horsepower was furnished by horses. It was not until early in the new century that machinery began to play a big role in our lives. The year was 1903 when the Wright brothers made their first flight in a heavier-than-air machine. Henry Ford's dream came true when he introduced the first Model T Ford in 1908. Still more years were to pass before transportation in America shifted from the steel rims of wagon and buggy to rubber tires.

At the turn of the century, the slaughter and exploitation of game birds, animals and fish had been a way of life with our growing nation, and our wealth of wildlife was in a sad state of devastation. The few restrictions passed by the Colonies, and later by the states, in the three hundred years since Jamestown was founded had not been enough to stop the carnage, but they were the initial steps toward the state and federal regulations that rescued some species from oblivion and created conditions that increased the range and numbers of others.

This was the decade that brought me on stage. My parents tell me I was born on Thanksgiving Day in 1906, and I am sure that as long as they lived, they tried to find something about me to be thankful for. My birthplace was no more than a settlement called Snapping Shoals, on the Newton-Henry county line in Georgia. I'm sure that the first music in my ears was the song of the Welaunee River—dubbed South River

by the white man—washing through the rocky flat and boulders that marked its course. Later, when I was a growing youngster, those shoals were my favorite water for catching catfish with a cane pole.

My first memories were of Oxford, Georgia, two miles above Covington. My family moved there when I was a toddler learning to walk and talk. Oxford was then the site of Emory University, which a few years later shifted its campus to a location near Atlanta.

Some of the memories of Oxford were so impressed on my immature mind that they remain vivid almost ninety years later. I remember the first electric light I ever saw, and my amazement when I pulled a cord and brought sunshine into a dark room. I was friends with several Emory College professors and especially one I knew as Dr. Peed (after ninety years I'm not sure of the spelling), who was the original absent-minded professor. Of the many stories told about his confusion, one was about the night he visited his next-door neighbor. When the visit was over and it was time to leave, the street was wrapped in a violent thunderstorm, with lightning and a torrential downpour. No rain gear was available, so the neighbor prevailed on Dr. Peed to spend the night. He agreed and shortly after disappeared. His hosts were still wondering what had happened when Dr. Peed came in out of the storm, completely drenched. He had gone home for his nightgown.

As related elsewhere, I started my hunting and fishing and my love affair with *Outdoor Life* while I lived at Oxford, and this was the beginning of a lifestyle and my life's work outdoors, a status from which I have never recovered.

In those years my father was a traveling salesman for a large produce company. From Oxford he covered several routes of country stores and was away from home four or five days each week. On these rounds my father traveled by horse and buggy. Henry Ford had introduced his first Model T in 1908, but the price of $850 for a gas buggy was far beyond the pocketbook of a grocery peddler who existed on small orders.

I made occasional day-long trips in the buggy with my father. He allowed me to carry along the latest copy of *Outdoor Life* for entertainment while I waited in the buggy. In those years *Outdoor Life* set a precedent of using stories from the best writers of the day and often about outdoorsmen well known to the average reader or who were on their way to

The Pardners —
"This is a good illustration of the miner's life in the Rockies. One is engaged in panning gold, while the other is wielding the rod in his endeavors to catch a mess of trout. A train on the Colorado Southern RY. is seen plying its way up the steep grade of the mountainside beyond."

becoming famous sportsmen. One example of this was their publication of the western hunting experiences of Theodore Roosevelt, who was elected president of the United States in 1901.

This decade provided one giant step in conservation. In 1903, Congress created the U.S. Bureau of Fisheries and, in 1905, passed laws that brought the U.S. Bureau of Biological Survey into existence. These departments were built on a solid foundation and remained as separate agencies until 1940, when they were combined into the U.S. Fish and Wildlife Service, which remains the chief federal conservation steward until this day.

The price for a copy of *Outdoor Life* in those years was 15¢.

A Goodly Bag of Birds —

"Me thinks I can see the fiendish, gleeful look that o'er spread his contenance as he discovers what is up...a large bunch of red heads...and a bunch of teal...came in and settled with my decoys."

From "Printers Ink vs. Wildfowl," by L.S. Day

1900

NEW YEARS EDITION

Outdoor Life

An Illustrated Monthly Magazine of Recreation *Published by* THE OUTDOOR LIFE PUBLISHING CO. Denver Colorado *Yearly Subscription.* $1.00 Single Copies 10 Cents

AUGUST, 1900.

Outdoor Life

A SPORTSMAN'S MAGAZINE OF THE WEST.

Published by THE OUTDOOR LIFE PUBLISHING CO., Denver, Colorado. Yearly Subscription $1.00, Single Copies 10 Cents.

Brown Palace Hotel, DENVER EUROPEAN & AMERICAN PLANS $1.50 & $3.00 PER DAY & UP

life

A SPORTSMAN'S MAGAZINE OF THE WEST
PUBLISHED BY THE OUTDOOR LIFE PUBLISHING CO., DENVER, COLO., YEARLY SUBSCRIPTION $1.00

CONQUEROR AND CONQUERED.
Monster Bear Killed in the Big Game Country near Marvine Lodge, Colo., by W. F. Purdy, of Meeker.

Boreas Post Office Under Snow —

"The Chimneys are all that can be seen of the house as it appeared in February, 1899. The postmaster stands over his undersnow passage leading to the house, the only means of ingress. The section house – a one and one-half story building – stands farther back, more than half covered with snow."

A Summer Idyll —

"The abandonment and freedom of the summer pleasure resort are fully exemplified in the accompanying picture...There is no doubt that the young woman represented in the picture...is an ardent enthusiast of the outdoor life, for we notice that she wears a smile and a happy face which would indicate that she is a participant in the pleasures of the forest and stream."

Waiting for a Bite —

"Winner of First Prize in *Outdoor Life's* August Photographic Competition."

A Three-Hour's Catch —

"On the way to Catalina it is no unusual thing for the boat to pass yellowtail, flying-fish, sunfish, shark, sword-fish and other strange denizens of the deep."

From "Fishing at Catalina," by G.E. Tuck

DECEMBER 1901

Ovtdoor life

HOLIDAY NUMBER, 15 CENTS.

IN THE SHEDDING TIME.

BROWN PALACE HOTEL, DENVER, ABSOLUTELY FIRE-PROOF
EUROPEAN & AMERICAN PLANS
$1.50 & $3.00 PER DAY & UP

JUNE 1901.   PRICE, 10 CENTS

Ovtdoor life

Fishing Number.

A SPORTSMAN'S MAGAZINE OF THE WEST $1.00
PUBLISHED BY THE OUTDOOR LIFE PUBLISHING CO., DENVER, COLO., YEARLY SUBSCRIPTION $1.00

FLYING FISH OF THE PACIFIC.

BROWN PALACE HOTEL, DENVER, ABSOLUTELY FIRE-PROOF
EUROPEAN & AMERICAN PLANS
$1.50 & $3.00 PER DAY & UP

Ovtdoor life

A SPORTSMAN'S MAGAZINE OF THE WEST $1.00
PUBLISHED BY THE OUTDOOR LIFE PUBLISHING CO., DENVER, COLO., YEARLY SUBSCRIPTION $1.00

BROWN PALACE HOTEL, DENVER, ABSOLUTELY FIRE-PROOF
EUROPEAN & AMERICAN PLANS
$1.50 & $3.00 PER DAY & UP

"This picture needs no explanation, as hundreds of homes have witnessed just such a return from the Spanish-American War."

Champion Ladies' Catch —

"The largest tuna ever taken at Santa Catalina Island, Calif., by a lady...also a good photograph of the captor."

An Old Man in Tattered Buckskin —

"His long gray hair flying from beneath an old beaver skin cap. In his right hand an old Hudson Bay gun, powder horn, bullet pouch, and long fringes flapping in the air."

From "Beaver Dick," by E.X. Paxson

Roping Antelope —

"While it is only under the rarest chance that an antelope or deer can be larieted...The practice, while affording rare excitement, is hardly sportsman-like, to say the least."

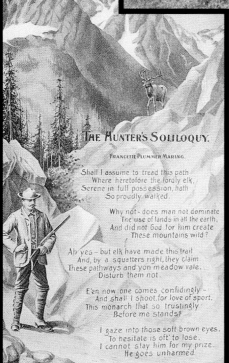

A California Big Tree —

" 'Smith's Cabin,' a great big tree in the Stanislaus group, the hollow base having been used in early years as a hunter's cabin."

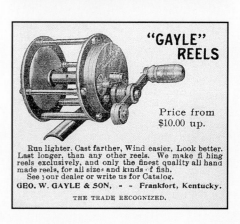

A Mixed Missouri Bag —

"Containing wild turkeys, 'possum, ducks, rabbits and lion."

Curiosity

Modern Mountain Beast of Burden —

"Showing Dick Rock of Lake, Idaho, his wife, and their tame moose hitched up ready to drive. [A sad calamity befell Mr. Rock since the above plate was made. During the past month he was gored to death by an enraged buffalo bull kept at his resort at Henry's Lake.—The Editor]"

The Battle

One Morning's Kill of Cats —

"We set our alarm clock so as to be up and ready at coming day...we would give the vermit our undivided attention, and furthermore that as hunting was what we sought, we would stay as long as the stock held out."

From "Hunting Cats in Texas," by L.L. Goodrich

"A California hunt – too heavy for one."

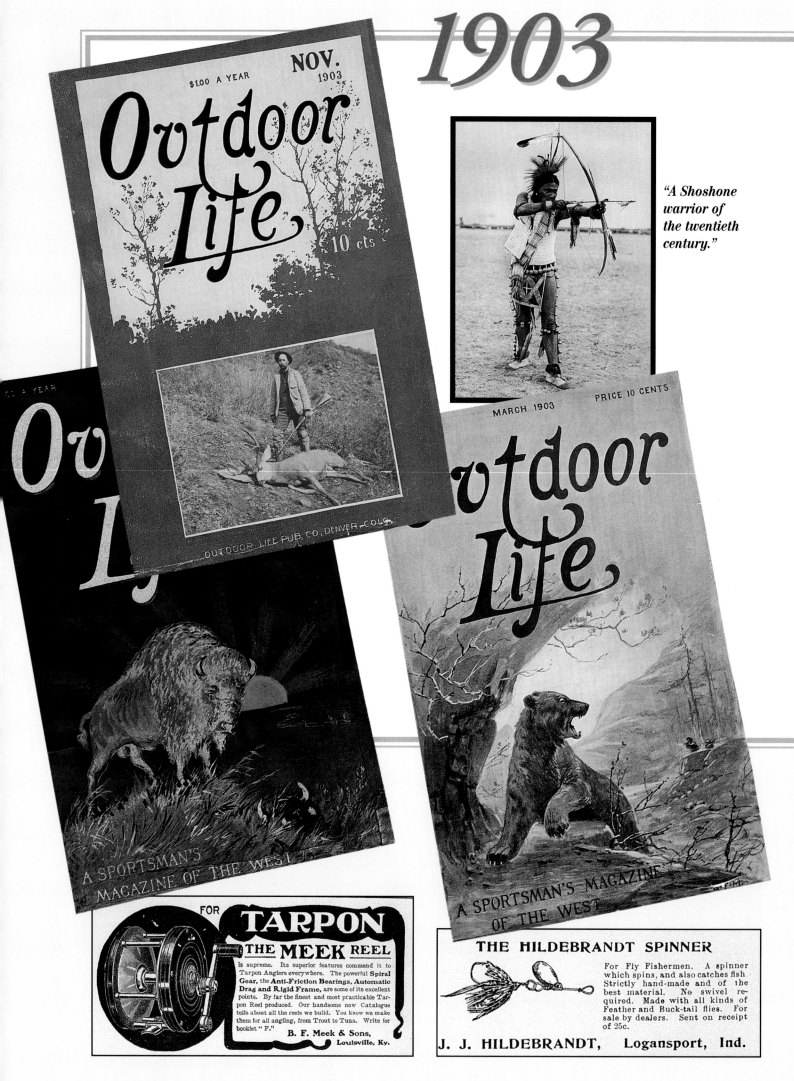

"A Shoshone warrior of the twentieth century."

NOV. 1903

$1.00 A YEAR

Ovtdoor Life

10 cts

OUTDOOR LIFE PUB. CO., DENVER, COLO

MARCH 1903   PRICE 10 CENTS

Ovtdoor Life

A SPORTSMAN'S MAGAZINE OF THE WEST

A SPORTSMAN'S MAGAZINE OF THE WEST

The New Browning Gun —

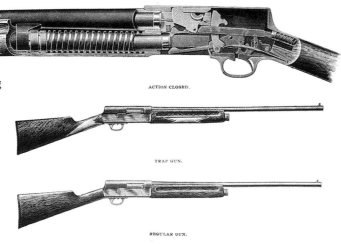

The Browning Automatic Shotgun.

ACTION CLOSED.

TRAP GUN.

REGULAR GUN.

"The invention of John M. Browning of Ogden, Utah, has just been placed on the market... Mr. Browning's new gun has all the earmarks of a winner."

From "The Month's Miscellany"

The Nymph's Blessing —

"Little Ione from a tree-clad bower
Came forth, a blossoming summer flower,
To place, as a plen-i-po-ten-sha-ree
A child's benediction in I-dyl-wee."

The Party and the Packs —
From "Devil's Den," by C.A. Meem D.D.S.

"Native–'Selling ammunition and sweetgoods, eh?'
Sportsman–'No, only on a ten-days' outing for deer.' "

1904

A Corner in** Outdoor Life's **Booth at the World's Fair —

"A glimpse into the corner of the booth maintained by this magazine at the St. Louis Exposition. It is located in space 34, Palace of Fish and Game, and is presided over by Miss Bessie Hortop, a typical western young lady, who will gladly welcome our friends visiting the fair."

Nebraska Sport and Sportsmen —

"Some of our readers may cry 'slaughter,' but if they will look at the number of hunters and consider that it took four days to kill these birds numbering about 100, they will of course realize that it is but moderate shooting."

The Proper Way to Pack a Deer —

"The accompanying photo shows what I consider the proper way to pack a deer...In this position the antlers are well protected and the legs will allow the horse to pass through thick timber."

From "Packing and Pack Animals," by Sam Stevens

"Mr. and Mrs. Colton as they drove into Pagosa Springs, Colorado, with their load of bear."

Stopped to Rest After a Long, Hard Pull —

"The scene portrayed is familiar to all deer hunters. Having killed a big buck miles from camp the entire party are dragging him in...in spite of the hard work, who would miss it?... weary and hungry, how much do you appreciate the supper of hot venison steaks, and stewed partridge, followed by an exchange of thought and stories of the chase."

1905

Outdoor Life

ROOSEVELT HUNT NUMBER

JULY 1905

PRICE 15 CENTS

Outdoor Life

DECEMBER 1905

PRICE 15 CENTS

Outdoor Life

NOV. 1905

PRICE 15 CENTS

The German Brown Trout —

"On a recent trip through the Yellowstone Park we cought from Shoshone Lake a new kind of trout, or at least new to us...He takes the fly freely and is a good fighter."
From "The German Brown Trout," by S.N. Leek

Examining Young Trout —
"The tub system at the Sutton Fish Hatchery."

A Woods-Nymph

"The President mounted on the Oregon horse, Fred."

The President on the road between New Castle and Glenwood Springs, as he was seen returning from his hunt.

From "The President's Bear Hunt," by John B. Goff

Deer Country —

"The Montana law allows the killing of six deer by each hunter in a season."

"Mountain goats killed at Glacier Station, on the W. P. & Y. Ry. by W.H. Case and Mr. Wafe."

The largest goat weighed 329 pounds and was 6 years old. The smallest weighed 250 pounds.

From "My Alaskan Trip," by Dr. J.W. Shults

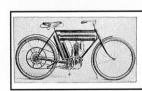

The Fair Duck Hunter

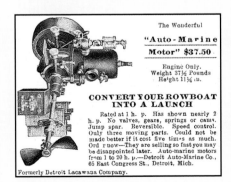

1906

The Demise of Four Toes —

"As the market quotations on bear pelts...were a trifle in excess of thirty dollars, and Mac's available assets ...being less than thirty cents, he determined to bag the bear."

From "The Demise of Four Toes," by F. W. Chase

"The limit on deer in the highlands of Ontario."
The Doner Hunt Club of Stayner, Ont. takes their limit, two a piece.

"I sneaked back an' dropped down back of a little weed an' watched."
From "Angling on Angel Creek," by N.H. Crowell

A Good Day for Fishing —
Atlantic coastline pier at St. Petersburg, Fla.

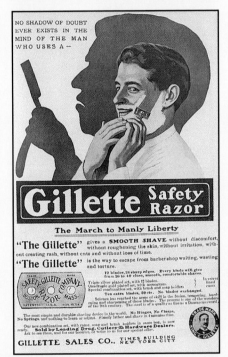

A California Jack-Rabbit Drive —
"The jack-rabbit...does damage each year to the extent of hundreds of thousands of dollars. He is therefore hunted...for the sole purpose of ridding the land of a very destructive enemy."
From "Driving the Jack-Rabbit," by Robert N. Reeves

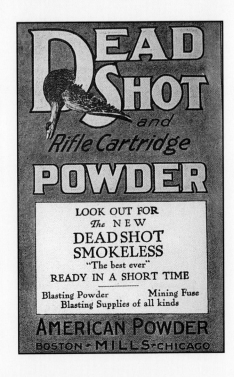

OUTDOOR LIFE
Oct. 1907 — Price 15¢

OUTDOOR LIFE
March 1907 — Price 15¢

OUTDOOR LIFE
Sep't 1907 — Price 15¢

GREGG

Labrador Musk Ox —

"...I explained to the factor that we wanted to get away into the interior to hunt and trap, and that I wanted to go to where musk ox could be found."

From "After Musk Ox in Labrador," by Hunter

"The tourist— 'I'm–ah–just over to kill a grizzly, don't cher know.' "

"The guide— who in all probability will do most of the killing."

The Decker Cabin – Our Headquarters —

"Ride as often and as far as you can, eat and drink everything placed before you, chop wood, sleep in the open, keep your head cool and your feet dry. Medicine, troubles, debts, Denver, all—forget 'em."

From "With the Big Game of Northwestern Colorado," by Theodore M. Brown

The Cimarron Terror —

"Some successful bear hunters of western Colorado–the Hotchkiss brothers–and a bear slain by them. This bear was a monster which had commited many depredations before being killed, and was known as the 'Cimarron Terror.' "

The Mountain Cowgirl —

"They are a fearless and beautiful type of American women–always happy and contented when astride a good saddler...They dress much the same as the cowboys and always consider the carbine and .45 Colt's an absolute necessity."

A Tuna Catch at Catalina Island —

From "An Island Autocracy," by Felix J. Koch

Outdoor Life *Editor, J.A. McGuire's Camp —*

"...ninety miles south of Cody, Wyo. His grizzly skin and elk antlers are to the right of the tent, while to the left is Fred Richard's big black bear hide, 7½ feet long–almost a record skin. Ned Frost is shown to the left of the picture with a magnificent set of elk horns, killed ten days before the author's arrival."

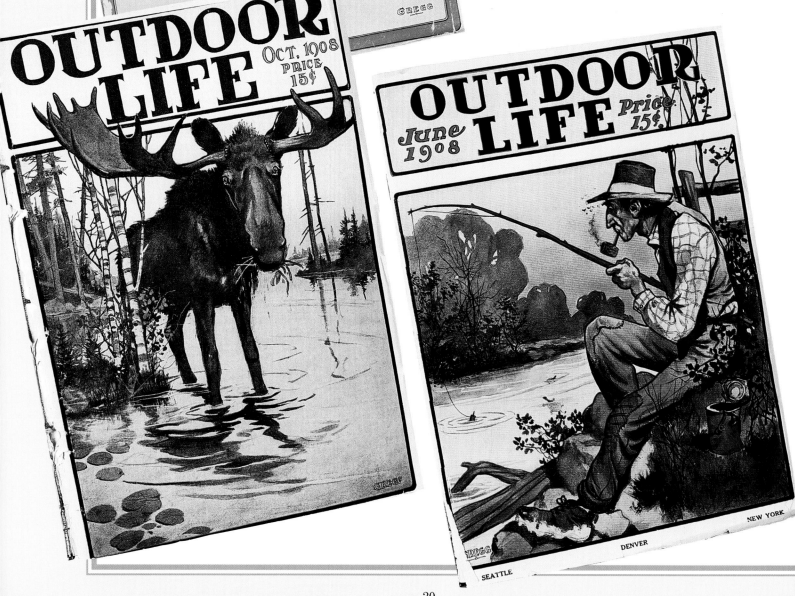

Caught on the Riffles —

"Scene on the Raging River, Wash., on the opening day of the season."

"Muskallonge caught in Lake Le Boeuf. The largest weighed 44lbs. 2oz."

From "Muskallonge Fishing in Pennsylvania," by A.J. Van Sise

Hunters and Their Trophies —

The author writes of hunting north of the Zambesi River while employed by the British South Africa Company.

From "The Big Game of Central Africa," by E.R. Murphy

Salmon Fishing in Seattle Harbor

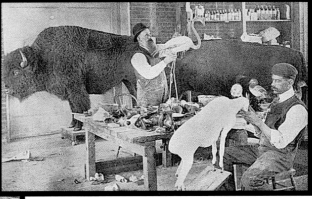

"The taxidermists at work on the specimens in the Denver Museum."
From "A Great Western Museum," by Papillo

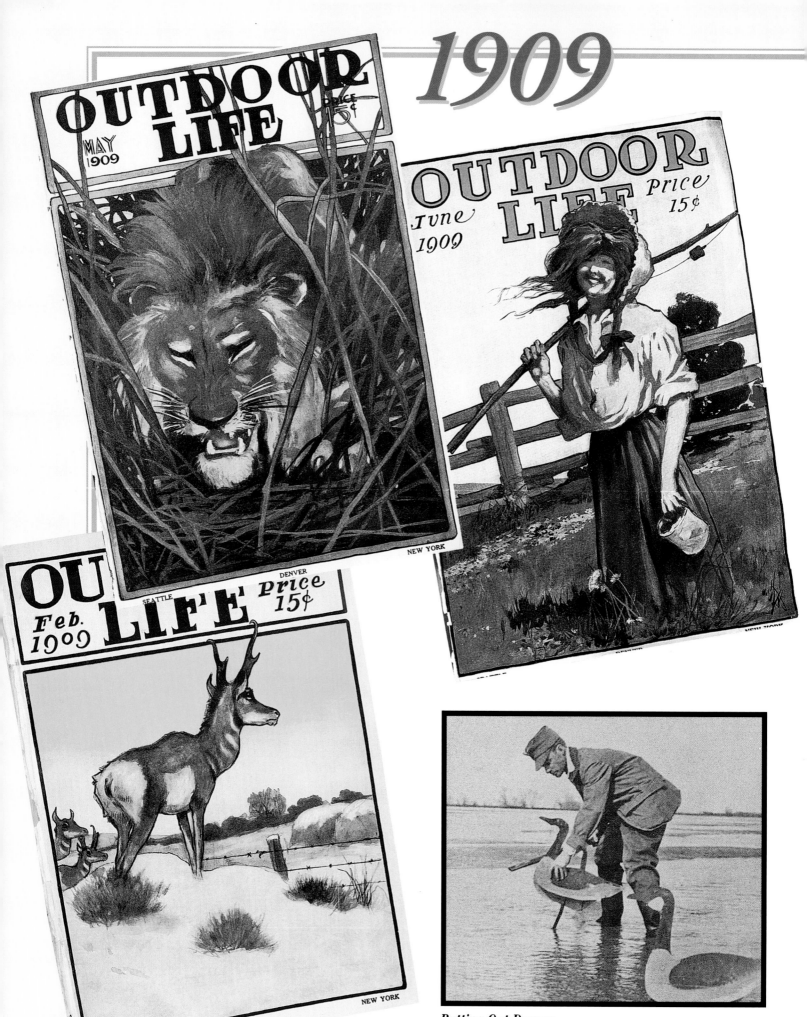

1909

OUTDOOR LIFE
MAY 1909
PRICE 15¢
NEW YORK

OUTDOOR LIFE
JVNE 1909
Price 15¢
DENVER   SEATTLE   NEW YORK

OUT LIFE
Feb. 1909
SEATTLE   DENVER   Price 15¢
NEW YORK

Putting Out Decoys —

"Goose shooting on the Platte river at Clarks, Neb."

Climbing toward the high, Bald
Caribou Range near the head of the
Klondike River in 40° below zero temps.
*From "A Hunter's Story of the Klondike,"
by Jack Lee*

As the Bear Fell —

"...Dr. J. Wylie Anderson, a homopathic physi-
cian and surgeon of Denver, recalls the climax
of his hunting career, killing the great brown
bear of Alaska, on Unimak Island."
*From "Hunting Ursus Gyas on Unimak," by Dr. J.
Wylie Anderson, M.D.*

A Diana in the Pheasant Fields —

*From "A Colorado Pheasant Farm,"
by J.A. McMahon*

An "Easy" Lion —

"A bullet from Mr. Webber's
.35-40 in the breast made a
'good' lion of it."

**"The unfortunate
hunter had his foot
caught in a twig
and fell prostrate."**

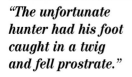

The Hunters, the Game
and the Dogs —

"My mind would wander to
thoughts of the possibilities
of a 'coon hunt on what
promised to be such an ideal
night for this sport."
*From "After the Coon Dogs in
Kansas," by Leon C. Rash*

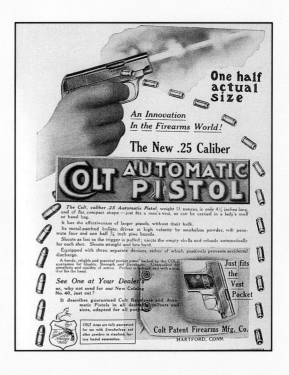

OUTDOOR LIFE

NOVEMBER
1910

LIFE

PRICE
15¢

L. MEGARGEE
1910

DENVER   SEATTLE   LOS ANGELES   NEW YORK

Best Of The *1910*s

WHEN I WAS FOUR YEARS OLD IN 1910, I DOUBT THAT I COULD HAVE CARED LESS THAT THE NATIONS OF THE WORLD WERE ON THE BRINK OF WORLD WAR I, OR THAT *OUTDOOR LIFE* HAD COME INTO EXISTENCE IN 1898, WAS EIGHT YEARS OLDER THAN I AND WAS MAKING ITS MARK AS AMERICA'S PREMIER HUNTING AND FISHING MAGAZINE.

I am sure that I spent little time in celebrating the fact that the lawmakers in my state were preparing legislation to be passed in 1911 to create the first fish and game department, with provisions for hunting and fishing seasons and bag limits and a license system to provide funds for operating the department and enforcing the new regulations.

Not until later, before I reached my teens and before the first World War, did I start bringing home bream and catfish from the little creek that ran behind our house and an occasional cottontail from one of the rabbit boxes "Uncle" Joe, a negro friend who worked a farm nearby, built for me and helped me set in the most productive places.

At that early age I was an avid reader of hunting and fishing stories and presume that *Outdoor Life* was my favorite magazine. I am sure that was when I began to live with my heroes who wrote or were a part of those adventures with mountain sheep, elk, the big bears and with fishing accounts from the creeks at timberline to the deep sea waters.

This decade is remembered for its part in World War I, but every bit as vividly

for its Eighteenth Amendment to the Constitution, which called for restriction on alcoholic beverages and was known simply as "Prohibition."

I am sure that as a teenager during the most of this decade, I was becoming aware through my own observation as well as through the pages of *Outdoor Life* that some of the game birds and animals found elsewhere no longer existed in my part of the state and were rare in other regions where they had once been abundant. The few deer in my state were found in the big river swamps, saltwater fringes and coastal islands. The range of our wild turkey had been reduced to isolated mountain coves, hunting plantations of the millionaire owners in the Southwest corner of the state and on the Atlantic coast.

As in most of the populated regions of the country, the hunting around my home in middle Georgia was limited to quail, rabbits, squirrels, migratory birds and some of the furry predators. This condition seems to have applied to most of the states except those blessed with vast wilderness regions.

Through the pages of *Outdoor Life* during this period, I became acquainted with William F. (Buffalo Bill) Cody. Though I never met Colonel Cody, I later knew many of his friends in Cody, Wyoming. One of these was "Phonograph" Jones, who worked for the famous frontiersman, and who, many years later, was my guide and cook on a sheep hunt in Yellow Creek Basin, next to the Thorofare. When I hunted with "Jonesy" he was in his nineties but could climb a mountain with a man half his age and wade the surging Shoshone River for half a day of fishing for trout.

Over a period of 25 years, I lived a total of many weeks on

the T. E. Ranch, which originally belonged to Colonel Cody but was owned by Robert W. Woodruff, president of The Coca-Cola Company. On the ranch, I hunted elk, mule deer and antelope, and I fished for trout in the North Fork of the Shoshone River while I lived in one of the cabins built many years before by Colonel Cody. I spent much time with Woodruff, in season and out. I considered him one of my best and most enjoyable friends.

My steps through the second decade of *Outdoor Life's* existence all seemed to point toward the years when I would become a member of the team that kept it the very best hunting and fishing magazine in the nation.

William Frederick Cody —

In describing the photo above, the author writes, "The man himself in private. A splendid example of the highest type of American manhood."

From "Buffalo Bill's Last Interview," by Chauncey Thomas

1910

A Big Moose Head from the Tanana Country —

"The largest head secured last season in the part of Alaska named. The spread is 62½ inches. Killed by J.B. Adams of British Columbia."

I.T. Alvord and his First Kadiak Bear Skin —

" 'They tell me, Moses [the author's guide], the bears are very bad to fight and kill men once in a while.' 'Dare not so berry bad,' said Moses, 'not if you kill dem quick.' "

From "The Big Bears of Kadiak Island," by I.T. Alvord

A Ball-Bearing Fishing Reel —

"It is claimed that an inexperienced person can learn bait casting more easily than with the ordinary multiplying reel."

From "A Ball-Bearing Fishing Reel," by Rollin Blackman

Here It Is
An Automobile
Within the Reach of all—$600

The car for which the World has waited. A high-grade, reliable business runabout. Costs less to keep than a horse and buggy—does the work of three.

When not in use expenses stop. A horse eats all the time—this MAXWELL is vastly more economical.

MAXWELL-BRISCOE MOTOR CO.
Main Office and Factory
WOOD STREET, TARRYTOWN, N. Y.
OTHER MAXWELL FACTORIES: New Castle, Ind., Pawtucket, R. I., Providence, R. I., Kingsland Point, N. Y.
LICENSED UNDER SELDEN PATENT

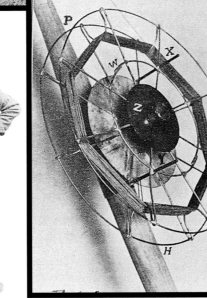

A Western Pistol Champion —

"Mr. Frank From...is one of the cleverest pistol and revolver shots in the West... He is a baker by profession and enjoys many outings during the hunting season in the pursuit of big game."

Mr. Penwell and his Family in the Car Used for Coursing Antelope —

"Detailing the excitement of a successful dash over the smooth Montana plains for the wary prong-horn in a modern motor car."

From "Antelope Hunting in an Auto," by John H. Raftery

WINCHESTER

THE RIFLE THAT HELPED PEARY REACH THE NORTH POLE

"Personally I always carry a Winchester rifle. On my last expedition I had a Model 1892 .44 caliber Carbine and Winchester cartridges, which I carried with me right to the North Pole. After I left the ship I depended upon it to bring down the fresh meat that we needed. Since 1888, both in Nicaragua and in the Arctic regions, I have always used the Winchester Repeaters. Each of my Arctic expeditions, since '91, has been fitted with these arms. The last expedition carried the .44-40 Carbine, for use on deer, seals, hare and the like, and the .40-82 for use on musk-oxen, walrus and polar bears. In facing the polar bears, in gathering a herd of musk-oxen with the least expenditure of time and price, less ammunition and in securing the greatest number of walrus out of an infuriated herd in the least time, I desire nothing better than a Winchester Repeater."
— COMMANDER ROBERT E. PEARY.

Winchester Guns and Ammunition,
the Red W Brand — are always

THE EQUIPMENT OF MEN OF ACHIEVEMENT.

The Four Archers Now Hunting Game in Alaska —

"Equipped as were the aborigines, these legal lights of Boston, Seattle and the Middle West will stalk their game and bring it down with the aid of only their 6-foot bows and 30-inch steel-tipped arrows."

From "Going Back to the Bow and Arrow," by Harry B. Richardson

Four Wild Buffalo Killed —

"From the last wild herd that roamed in Lost Park until 1897. They were killed illegally and concealed for taxidermy purposes."

From "Mounted Specimens of the Last of the Wild Buffalo"

A Monster Alaskan Bear and Its Captor —

"Dr. J. Wylie Anderson and the mounted skin of an Alaska Grizzly bear that he killed while on a hunting trip on Unimak Island, Alaska. The mounted skin measuring 11 feet long and the weight being over 1300 pounds."

F.E. Kleinschmidt and Polar Bear, Bering Sea —

"Perhaps it's not alluring to you to spend the winter among the eskimos; travel a hundred or two hundred miles by dog team from Nome or Teller; build an ice-hut; live on crackers and frozen meat with an eskimo as companion; go out on the drifting floe ice for days and weeks before it is your great fortune to get a bear."

From "Game Notes from Alaska," by F.E. Kleinschmidt

Mr. J.W. Garlic and His Big Buck —

"Killed in Kittitas County, Ore., while on a hunting trip with Mr. A.D. Case, this buck dressed in at over 200 pounds. Both men killed the law's allowance of deer within 48 hours' ride from town."

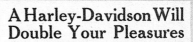

The Car "In Camp" —

"Mr. Du Pont's outfit is one of the most complete and elaborate combinations yet accomplished, and he takes great pleasure in the use of it."

From "Mr. Du Pont Originates a Real Camp Car," by Ernest Coler

1912

OUTDOOR
LIFE
MAY
1912
PRICE
15¢
CLARENCE
ELLSWORTH

OUTDOOR
LIFE
AUG.
1912
PRICE
15¢

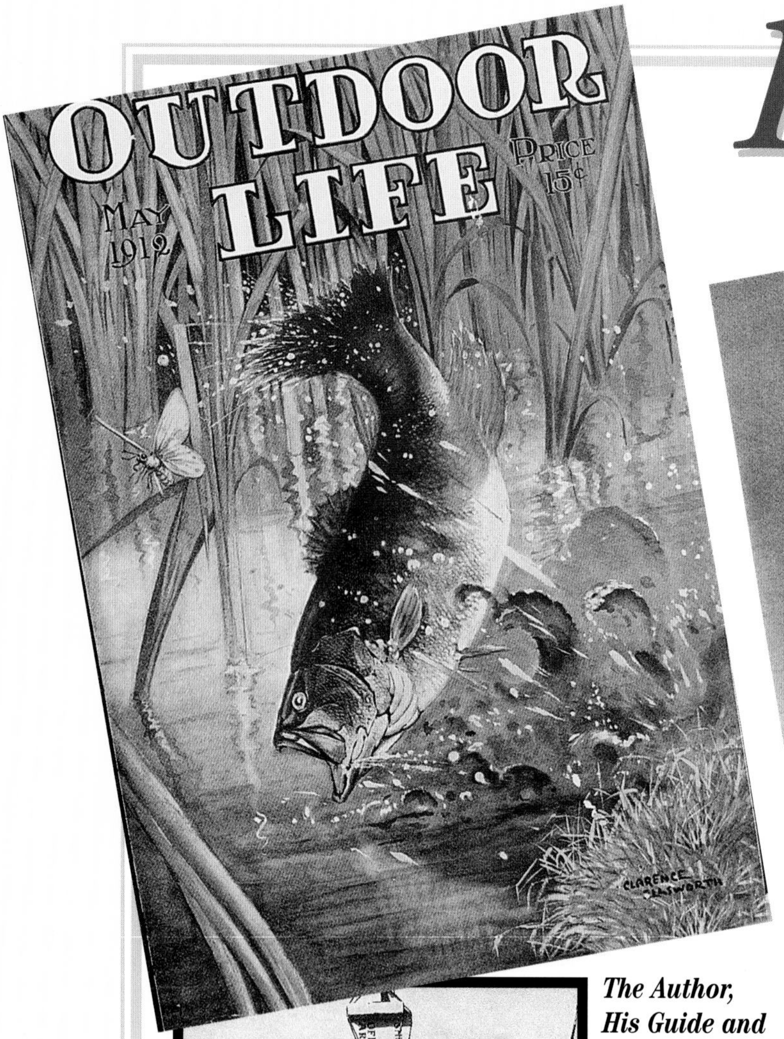

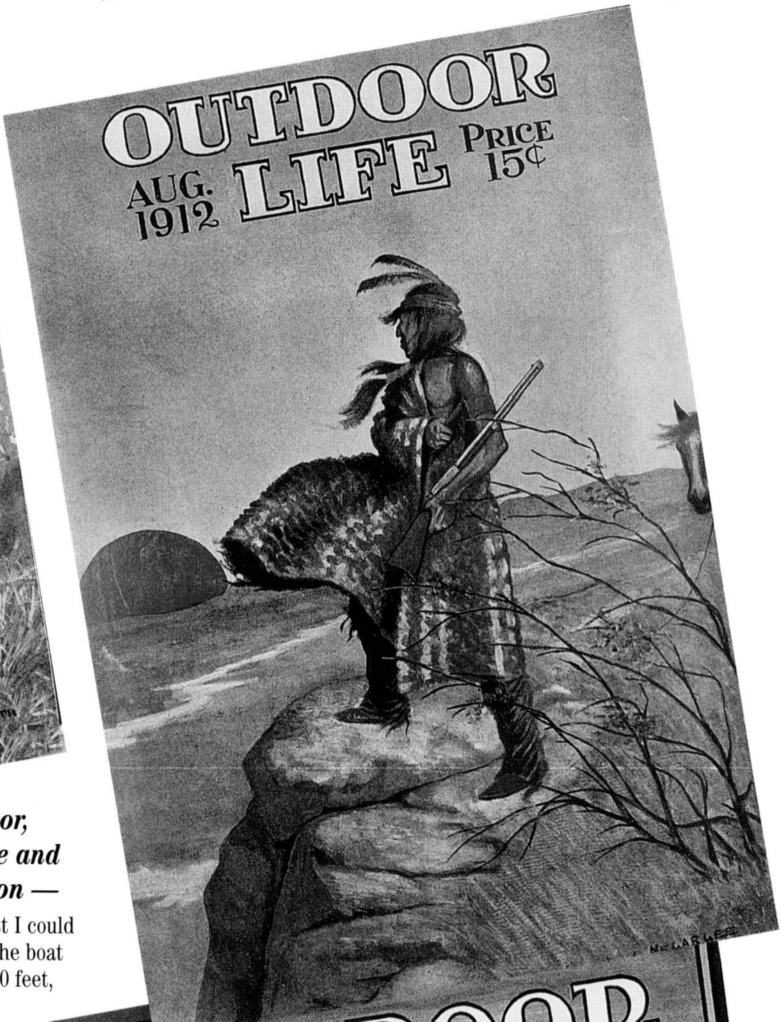

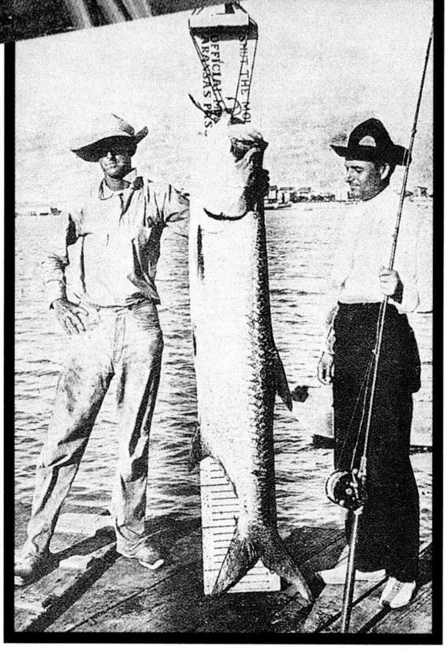

The Author, His Guide and His Tarpon —

"The nearest I could get him to the boat was about 60 feet, but I had tired him out, and was only too glad when we had him on shore, for I was all in. He weighed over 100 pounds and measured 5 feet 10 inches."

From "Exciting Sport at Tarpon Fishing," by C.C. Hildebrand

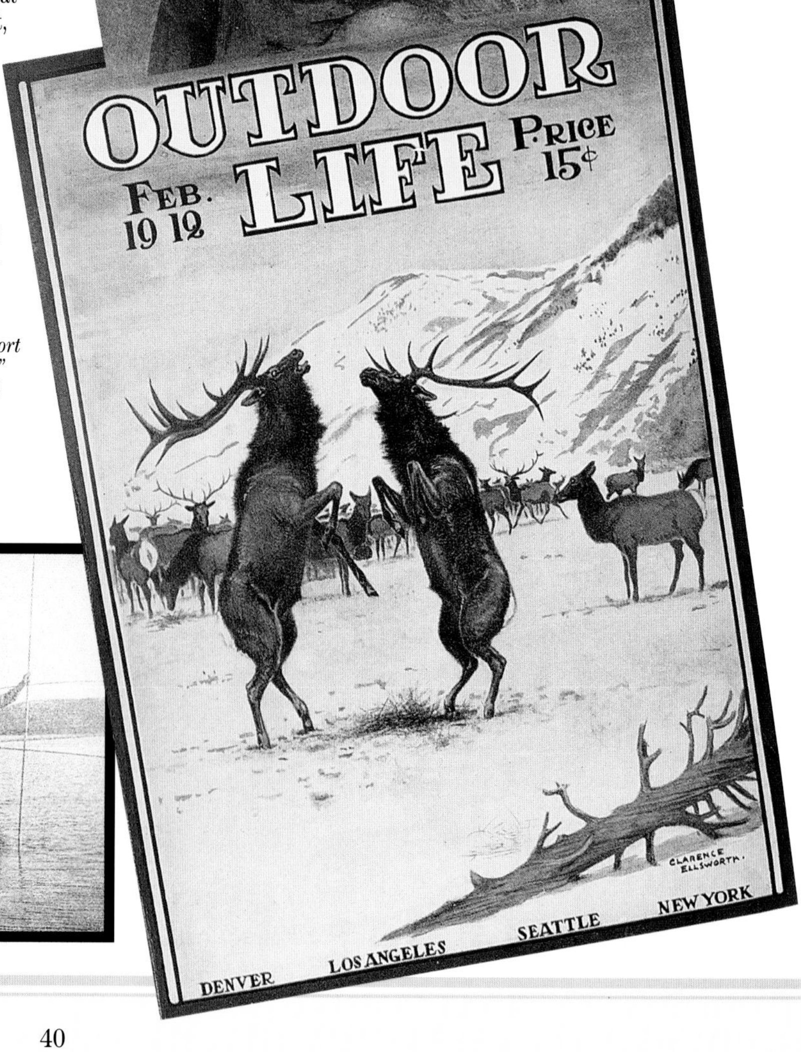

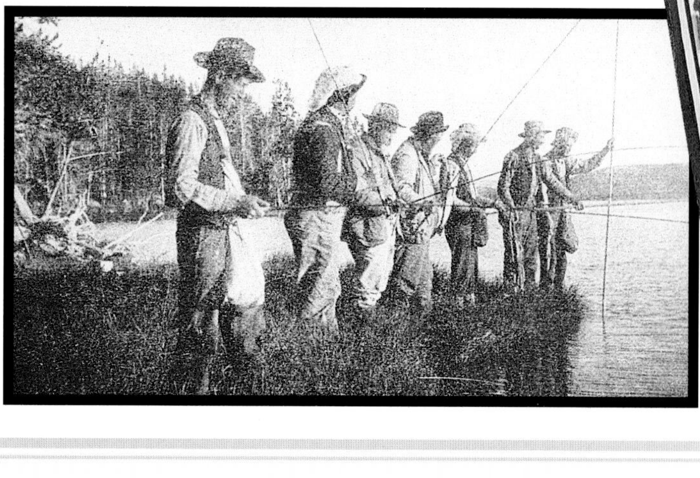

OUTDOOR
LIFE
FEB.
1912
PRICE
15¢
CLARENCE
ELLSWORTH
DENVER
LOS ANGELES
SEATTLE
NEW YORK

When Fishing Is Good in Jackson Hole

Mr. Humphrey and Ram with Finest Head —

"We had not gone ten steps when a pair of big horns suddenly popped up over a little ridge not more than eighty yards away. The ram immediately jumped on top of a large boulder and stood looking at us. He was a magnificent picture, and his large, yellow horns glittered in the sunlight."

From "Shooting the Vanishing Sheep of the Desert," by W.E. Humphrey

Kaw-Cloa, a Thlinget Maiden from Chilkoot

Capt. F.E. Kleinschmidt with Seal and Walrus Head —

"It has been my custom every spring shortly after the breaking up of the ice to take a number of friends out for a cruise after seal or walrus."

From "An Arctic Motor Cruise," by Capt. F.E. Kleinschmidt

The Author with a String of Trout —

"Time was made to fish for trout amid hunting blackbear, trapping rats and braving the rapids of the Croche."

From "A Spring Hunt in Quebec," by Capt. N.B. Harrington

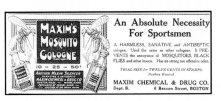
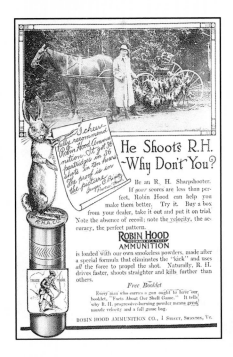

Male Tiger, "One Fang" Killed in Mexico, Dec 21, 1910 —

"As to his man-eating propensities I have no proof; but I can testify in person that he will attack man, having experienced one's charge on this very trip. The first jaguar we secured, in fact was shot in mid air while springing upon one of our party, the distance being so close that the impact of the animal's dead body knocked the shooter down."

From "Jaguar Hunting in Old Mexico," by Scott Teague

Hunting Ducks from an Aeroplane —

"This photograph is of a record-breaking duck shoot from a hydro-aeroplane...Seventeen ducks were killed in a few minutes by shooting them as they flew by."

A Single Elephant Tusk Over 11 Feet Long —

"My own inclination is to class the elephant as the most dangerous...A dropping shot is almost entirely out of the question, and when wounded they have the nasty knack of looking to see who did it."

From "Elephant Hunting – The Classic of Sport," by W. Robert Foran

Eskimos Hunting Walrus —

From "Alaska, Her Game and Game Laws," by Capt. F.E. Kleinschmidt

A Canal Zone Hunting Club in the Field —

"The American workers on the great ditch have formed hunting clubs and imported hounds from the United States, and every Sunday dogs and men leave the noisy canal behind and invade the silent jungle."

From "A Canal Zone Game Preserve," by Crede Haskins Calhoun

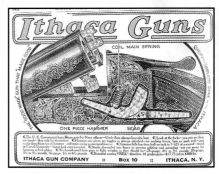

1914

OUTDOOR LIFE

FEBRUARY ~ 1914 ~

PRICE 15¢

OUTDOOR LIFE

AUG. 1914

PRICE 15¢

OUTDOOR LIFE

APRIL 1914

Mounted Specimen of Passenger Pigeon Owned by M.J. Young —

"As far as I am able to learn they are entirely extinct, and we have the market hunter to blame for it."

From "One Living Passenger Pigeon Left," by M.J. Young

Kermit Roosevelt and Maned Lion —

"...keep on firing so long as there is sign of life in his body, for once a lion charges he will not stop until either you or he is dead."

From "A Mix-Up with a Troop of Lions," by J. Alden Loring

A Pelican from Utah —

"Rogers and Valentine, two enthusiastic Utah sportsmen, holding a pelican measuring 7 ft. 6 in. tip to tip, killed by one of their party, O.W. McGill."

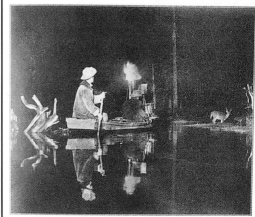

Mr. Thomas and the Big Sting-Ray —

"The huge sea denizen weighed 80 pounds and was the dimensions of a tub."

From "Landing a Monster Sting-Ray," by E.W. Thomas

Everything Moves on Sleds —

Winter fishing for the Rocky Mountain whitefish on Lake Oreille.

From "Winter Fishing,"
by Charles Stuart Moody, M.D.

OUTDOOR LIFE JULY 1915 PRICE 15¢

OUTDOOR LIFE NOV 1915 PRICE 15¢

OUTDOOR LIFE JAN. 1915 PRICE 15¢

A Morning's Bag of Tigers by the Maharajah —
"The second from the left, one of the largest ever shot in India."

A Nepalese Rhino Brought Down in the Jungle —
"...the jungle grass grows in places higher than the howdahs of the elephants."

Annihilation

Lee's Two Fine Heads —
"They measured 13¾ and 12¼ inches at base."
From "Hunting Big Game in Alaska," by J.R. Ferrell

1916

Mirroring Nature —

"Copy with your fly the appearance and action of the natural insect."

From "Holding the Mirror up to Nature – On a Trout Stream," by Samuel G. Camp

The Largest Tarpon on Record —

"Weight, 101 lbs. Caught on the Gatun Spillway while the gates were open, and with light tackle."

From "Our New Hunting Country: Part IV, The Fishing," by Lieut. Townsend Whelen

A Proud Turkey Hunter —

"The turkey hunter is a proud man when success crowns his efforts."

The Little Black Dog Had the Situation in Hand —

"...with a team of five dogs, James Brace, Don McMillan and I left for the floe after bear."

From "After Bears," by Frank C. Hennessey

Mack and Two Goats —

"As Lee and I were only a short distance apart at this time, he whistled at me and waved his hat that he was off for his goat."

From "In Alaska's Game Retreats," by J.R. Farrell

MARCH 1917 OUTDOOR LIFE **PRICE 15¢**

MAY 1917 OUTDOOR LIFE **PRICE 15¢**

BUFFALO BILL'S LAST INTERVIEW

SEPT. 1917 OUTDOOR LIFE 15¢

CHARLIE BARKER MASTER WOODSMAN BY TOWNSEND WHELEN

Catalina Island Tuna —

"Caught by G.W. Hooper at Catalina Island, Cal., September 30, 1916. Weights, reading from left to right, 74 lbs., 100 lbs. and 92¾ lbs."

From "Avalon – A Gem in the Pacific," by Fred Bradford Ellsworth

A Columbia River Sturgeon —

"This gigantic fish measured eleven feet and three inches, was sixty-four inches in circumference, and weighed 750 pounds. It contained 127 pounds of caviar valued at 35 cents per pound..."

From "A Big Columbia River Sturgeon," by O.W. Smith

Buffalo Bill by Rosa Bonheur—

"This is the only picture of a man on horseback she ever painted. [the original] Worth $10,000 when done, and now valued at $40,000."

From "Buffalo Bill's Last Interview," by Chauncey Thomas

A Giant Sea Bass —

A world record bass weighing 493 lbs., caught by N.A. Howard of California at Avalon.

A Battery Gun —

"One shot fired into bedded water fowl could easily result in the killing of 100 birds. And to think that such engines of destruction to our game are even made, much less used, in a civilized country the size and standing of this!"

The Motorcycle Used in Massachusetts Deer Hunting —

A motorcycle was used to transport the hunter and his 250-lb. buck home after a weekend hunt in Massachusetts. The buck was killed with a single-barrel shotgun because deer hunting with a rifle in Massachusetts was prohibited.

"The happy hunters and their slick-looking deer."

From "Deer Hunting in South Dakota," by John T. Lutey

1918

Braving the Rapids for Bear —

"He was a tower of strength as he grasped the sweep with his powerful hands, his wonderful eyes glued on the white mass of foam ahead."

From "Thru the Heart of the Bitter Roots: Part IV," by Ralph Edmunds

Outdoor Life
DEC. 1918
PRICE 20¢

THE LIFE OF AN ELK BY S.N. LEEK

Outdoor Life
APRIL, 1918   PRICE 20¢

IN THE ONTARIO MOOSE FIELDS - M.C. JOHNSTON, M.D.
THE GAME FIELDS OF THE CASSIARS - POWHATAN ROBINSON

Outdoor Life
MAR. 1918
20¢ A COPY

COLORADO TRAILS, ZANE GREY
SINGLE HOOKS, OR GANGS - ROBERT PAGE LINCOLN

A Feat Worthy of Much Eulogy —

"...imagine yourself miles out upon the beautiful turquoise sea...in tow by the greatest exhibition performer of salt water, a crafty silver king."

From "Angling for the Silver King in the Gulf of Mexico," by H.M. Hampton

The Automobile in the Game Fields —

"While hunting deer in an automobile is perfectly legitimate and lawful, yet it is sad to reflect that the automobile is slowly but surely causing a big shrinkage in our game – both horned and feathered."

"Now, why the dickens couldn't I find youse the other day when I wanted to go fishin'?"

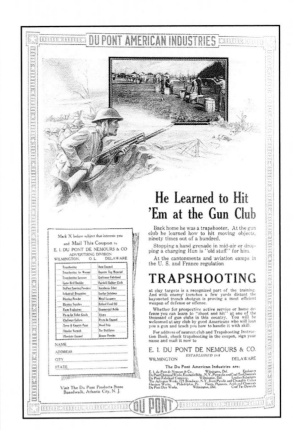

1919

Outdoor Life
JAN. 1919   PRICE 20¢

FOUR BEARS IN 15 MINUTES BY OSCAR WARD
IN THE CLOUDS BY GRACE M. HARVEY
Howard L. Hastings

Outdoor Life
20¢ A COPY   JUNE 1919

HITTING THE HIGH SPOTS IN WYOMING" BY C.E. SYKES
THE BEAR HUNTING EXPERIENCES OF A GUIDE" BY CHAS. H. BAXTER

Outdoor Life
PRICE 20¢
DEC. 1919

WITH THE WILDFOWL OF BARNEGAT — F.A. WILLITS
IN THE REALM OF THE SOURDOUGH — J.A. McGUIRE
Howard L. Hastings

The Author and Brown Bear —

"I gave him the second ball in the air and the third and fourth
as he rushed up and the fifth stopped him within a few feet."

*From "Killing a Flock of Brown Bears in Alaska,"
by Capt. F.E. Kleinschmidt*

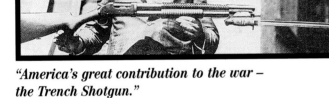

*"America's great contribution to the war –
the Trench Shotgun."*

Outdoor Life

MAY 1921

PRICE 25¢

KINDS OF FIRE AND THEIR USES—F.H.Cheley
10,000 MILES TO ALASKA FOR MOOSE AND SHEEP—T.R.Hubback

Best Of The 1920s

BEFORE THE BEGINNING OF *OUTDOOR LIFE'S* THIRD DECADE, I HAD LIVED THROUGH THE "BENT PIN" ERA BUT WAS NEVER A MEMBER OF THAT CULT WHO SOMEHOW TWISTED STRAIGHT PINS INTO CURVES THAT WOULD HOLD A WORM OR CRUST OF BREAD BUT SELDOM A FISH.

When I was old enough to steal and to toddle to the creek behind our house, I filched enough coins out of my mother's change purse to purchase "store-bought" fish hooks and lead sinkers, and I appropriated enough heavy sewing thread to arrange my tackle on the fishing pole cut from a stand of bamboo on the creek bank. My rig was heavy enough to land any bream or catfish I hooked in the little creek.

This was the beginning of my life in the woods, waters and outdoors of two continents and my first step toward the dedication of my entire existence to the world beyond four walls. This includes that part of my earthly journey when, for half a century or more, I walked the trail with *Outdoor Life.*

It might be considered high treason to admit that I do not remember the first time I ever saw a copy of *Outdoor Life.* Nor can I recall the time when I did not eagerly await the postman on that day when my favorite magazine was due to arrive. I know that I was old enough to read with understanding and not have to confine my pleasure to only looking at the pictures.

I did not limit my earliest outdoor activities to fishing. I was also a very active hunter. My first sporting arm was a BB gun, my first quarry the English sparrow. The English sparrow had been introduced into this country in the early 1850s. Why, no one was ever able to explain. In

the 1800s and well into the 1900s these alien sparrows, with our vast horse population to feed them, increased until they became a nuisance, and there was no objection when I did a few of them in. My young imagination transformed every sparrow I stalked and waylaid into a wild turkey or Canada goose, and I learned quickly never to point that gun, loaded or unloaded, in the direction of any person. Fortunately there was no limit on English sparrows.

At some period in those early years I learned from the pages of *Outdoor Life* that hunting was confined by seasons and limits and that men who wore badges were around to see that those restrictions were observed.

My home state of Georgia had passed its first game law in 1790 to stop the killing of deer at night with the use of a light, and in 1891 enacted a general law that allowed no hunting at certain seasons of the year for deer, wild turkey, and grouse (known locally as pheasant).

Before, and early in the 1900s, most states set up game laws with departments to administer them. Georgia's first game warden system was created in 1903 with a Game and Fish Commission to supervise the officers.

During this decade most of the states, with the support and promotion of *Outdoor Life* and other hunting and fishing magazines, had helped develop sportsmen's organizations to support the growing conservation movement and completely eliminate the unchecked slaughter of game birds and animals that had plagued our nation for almost three centuries.

The records indicate that when *Outdoor Life* was founded in 1898 by John A. McGuire, his silent partner in the venture

was J. A. Ricker, who was publishing his own magazine, *Outdoor Recreation.* McGuire and Ricker were close friends, and both publications continued as separate magazines until 1927, when they merged into *Outdoor Life & Outdoor Recreation.* The result was a vastly increased circulation, a much larger office force and a new staff of prominent and popular authors.

Editor McGuire was enthusiastic about the merger. He stated that the combined magazine would continue "the practical influence it has wielded in legislative and game conservation councils . . . will show how far devotion to wild game and the average citizen's enjoyment of that game, has motivated the publication . . . What was more important was the widening of *Outdoor Life's* circulation, which furnished the means of preaching game protection to larger audiences."

Editor McGuire went on to say that "In the matter of conservation, we shall be fearless—and fair. The arms, powder and tackle manufacturers welcome, the reader enjoys, and both state and national

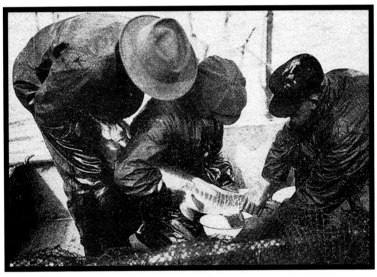

Spawning a Muskellunge (1925) —
"Insofar as I know the only successful 'lunge [spawning] station now in operation is that at Chautauqua, New York, where I am informed considerable is accomplished . . ."
From " 'Lunge," by O.W. Smith

officials are influenced by a *bold* magazine. Experience shall be our background, specialized authorities our counselors, persistency the goal with which to induce actiòn—and YOU, Mr. Sportsman, in the future as in the past, shall be the Judge."

Outdoor Life in massive type continued to dominate the covers, with *Outdoor & Recreation* in smaller print. This was finally discontinued in the early 1930s.

1920

Outdoor Life

OCTOBER 1920   PRICE 25¢

A QUAIL HUNT IN ARKANSAS—H.C.Stinson
IN THE LAND OF THE MIDNIGHT SUN—C.E.Sykes

Outdoor Life

NOVEMBER 1920   PRICE 25¢

HUNTING IN THE FLORIDA CYPRESS SWAMPS—W.M.GARLINGTON
A MUSEUM COLLECTING TRIP TO THE NORTH—Dr.EDW.D.JONES

MARCH 1920   PRICE 20¢

ON THE MOOSE TRAIL IN NEW BRUNSWICK By CYRUS THOMPSON
CHARGED BY A BLACK BEAR, By C. M. CARSON

51 Lb. 3 Oz.
Muskie —

"Go ye, now, into the wilderness and play in God's Great Outdoors... Drink in the vitalizing, pure, pine-laden air... Catch plenty 'beeg' muskellunge with 'light tackle' and return to the water all fish caught except those needed for food, or one desired for mounting."

From "Tigers of the Fresh Waters," by Fred Bradford Ellsworth

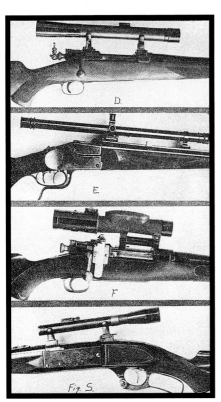

Some Rifle Telescopes —

"A comprehensive treatise on a shooting accessory that should come into more popular favor."

From "The Rifle Telescope," by J.R. Bevis, M. Sc., Ph.D.

Dr. Chase and his Big Brown Bear Skin —

"He could not very well be moved as his weight was estimated at from 1,600 to 1,800 pounds. With an ax they had to chop out pieces of the bear in order to remove the skin."

From "Killing a Mammouth Alaska Bear"

Tarpon and Shark —

"The author's 165 lb. tarpon and the 800 lb. shark that were landed on this trip. The part of the tarpon taken from the shark's belly is shown above the shark."

From "The Tale of the Tarpon," by Dr. J. Barney Low

A Day's Catch —

"After catching a number of cut-throats in Lake Quinault, Washington, the author and his fishing companions fish the Satsop River and catch a 34-inch rainbow."

From "Capturing a Big Rainbow on the Satsop," by Charles E. Myers

Three Gulf Coast Tarpon —

"Caught these three and then quit in order to get dinner."

From "On Florida's Waterways in Winter," by Joseph W. Stray

Outdoor Life *Reduces Its Subscription Price*

Outdoor Life

NOVEMBER 1922
20¢

Howard L. Hastings

ECOYING WILD TURKEYS — Dr. B. T. Jones

A Contribution to Antelope Preservation —
The American Bison Society of Alberta, Canada, transplants antelope to game preserves throughout the western United States.

Ou **Outdoor Life**

JANUARY 1922

PRICE 20¢

APRIL 1922

20¢

THE GRAVE OF BUFFALO BILL—
BY CHAUNCEY THOMAS
KODAK SHOTS OF HUNTING IN THE FAR NORTH
BY WM. T. YOUNG

H. L. HASTINGS

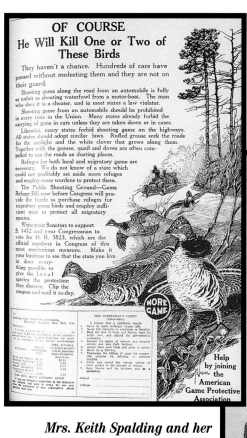

Hunting Ethics —

This message from the American Game Protective Association calls for hunters to stop road-hunting for game.

Mrs. Keith Spalding and her 426-Pound Broadbill —

"To see a big fish hooked on your line, and then watch the monster's head and fins dash from one place to another, gives one a thrill very difficult to describe. I do not think I could land a 400-pound tuna; but some time, if the opportunity should arise, I shall probably try to do so."

From "Angling Thrills – A Swordfish Story," by Ernest Windle

A Bear and Three Eagles —

The author, left in the photo above, with his guide and a big Alaskan brown bear. The three eagles he shot, right photo, were taken "incidentally" while bear hunting.

From "Hunting the Big Big Brown Bears of Alaska," by Gus Peret

1923

A GAME PARADISE OF THE CANADIAN ROCKIES – J.H.Estes
SIWASHING IN SIBERIA – John B.Burnham

SHOOTING AFRICAN GAME BY PROXY – Chas. Cottar
IN THE MOOSE FIELDS OF QUEBEC – L.R. Wyckoff

"A ring-necked 'greenhead,' sometimes called a mallard drake."

The author tells of an October morning in 1922 when he spotted a long V-shaped string of Canada geese flying overhead at the exact moment he was kissing his wife good-bye before leaving for work. The two decide to skip the responsibilities of the day and take their sidecar to the San Marino marshes in California to hunt waterfowl.

From "Hunting in the San Marino Marshes," by Edwin Hogg

Here's to the Girl —

"Here's to the Girl of the big out-of-doors,
The girl of the rifle and reel;
She's out when it's sunny, she's out when
it pours,
With waders and fly-rod and creel.

Here's to the Girl of the forest and field
In khaki and knockabout hat:
Her cheeks may be tanned and her nose
may be peeled,
But we love her the more for all of that!

She can cook on a fire of hickory coals,
She's able to drink from a jug;
She never complains that the tent's full
of holes,
And she isn't afraid of a bug.

Her hardships and worries are never revealed,
When troubled, she smiles her way through;
So here's to my sweetheart of forest and field,
You guessed it! My wife – here's to you!"

By Sherman Ripley

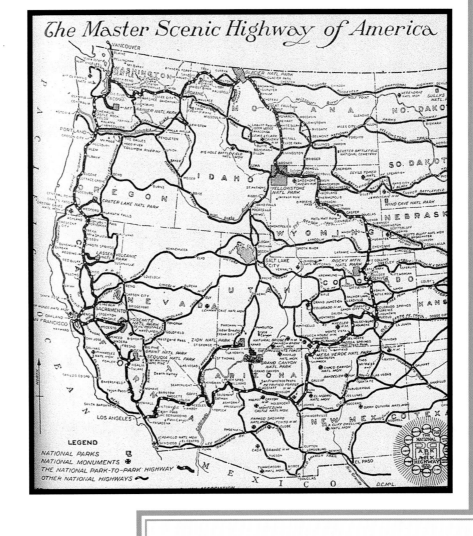

The Master Scenic Highway of America

LEGEND
NATIONAL PARKS
NATIONAL MONUMENTS
THE NATIONAL PARK-TO-PARK HIGHWAY
OTHER NATIONAL HIGHWAYS

Time to Quit —

"Are these enough to fill that emptiness–with all the fixin's?"
From "When Autumn Leaves Are Falling," by Jack Maxwell

1924

Outdoor Life

JANUARY 1924
20¢

Outdoor Life

MAY 1924   20¢

AN ALASKAN HUNT FOR SHEEP, BEARS, and CARIBOU—John B. Burn
A DESIRABLE TENT WHEN GOING LIGHT—Ashley A. Haines.   Howard

OCTOBER 1924   20¢

IN THE DOMAIN OF THE BIG HORN—R. M.
BULL MOOSE—R.
SBORNE
AYER

Returning to Camp with Cape and Horns —

"He was walking and sixty yards away. I drew my bow till the 3-inch steel head on the 28-inch arrow touched my finger, then released. The flight of the arrow seemed perfect for a good hit."

From "Hunting Moose with the Bow and Arrow," by Arthur H. Young

U.S. Hunter in Fur —

"...in olden times people used to have dyspepsia; now they call it gastritis. It is the same thing, but the new name sounds nicer. Well in olden times I would have been called a trapper."

From "On the Trail with Our Government Trappers," by M.D. Orange

The Big Boy —

"There have been stories of the killing of big bears and bigger bears, but in this account is recorded the demise of the biggest bear ever taken by any sportsman so far as it is known."

From "The Fall of the King of Kadiaks," by Ira A. Minnick

1925

Outdoor Life
APRIL 1925
20¢

Outdoor Life
FEBRUARY 1925
20¢

AFTER BEARS WITH BAXTER . . . . EDISON MARSHALL
WYOMING ELK AND BIGHORN   G. SCOTT TOWNE, M.D.

Outdoor Life
DECEMBER 1925
20¢

TACKLE HIM, HANK!

AN old-timer like you is too
slow for football!"
"Shoot Hercules E. C. and
Infallible and you won't have
to chase cripples."

Write for free copies of our
publications, *The Shooter's
Guide*, *Field and Trap Shooting* and *A Talk About Sporting Powders*.

Hercules Powder Company
902 King Street
Wilmington   Delaware

"The bitter bit; showing how a bass's eye may be larger than its mouth."
From "Bass Lore," by O.W. Smith

A Lucky "Day" for Sailfish —

"Mr. Clark Day...landed a record sailfish after fighting it for an hour...the fish weighed 102 pounds and measured 8 feet 4 inches after it was dry."

King Silver King —

"A 190-pound tarpon captured by Mr. Iven on an 18-thread line and an 11-ounce split bamboo rod. This is the world's record on tackle of that weight."

From "Landing a 190-Pound Silver King on an 18-Thread Line," by C.J. Iven

Outdoor Life

JANUARY 1926
20¢

BEN TINKER
DR. J. A. WIBORN

Outdoor Life

MAY 1926
20¢

DREAMS THAT CAME TRUE ALMOST   DR. CHARLES H. MOORE
WITH THE BIG STICK   A. F. WESTERVELT

Outdoor Life

AUGUST 1926   20¢

To Far Western Alaska for Big Game (Part 3) . . . . T. R. Hubback
Black Bass and Feather Minnows . . . . O.W. Smith

Drawing the Bow & (right) Arrows Driven Thru ¾ Inch of Teakwood at 40 Yards —

"...you will find, upon reading this article, that the properly made outfit passes from a toy into a weapon...Its accuracy and killing power in the hands of an expert archer are indeed remarkable."

From "Archery – Sport, Pastime, Man-Builder," by Earl B. Powell

spring fever

tho the windows still are frosted
and the winds still bluster keen
I do not see the sleet glazed panes
nor the pavements icy sheen.
the sun has pierced the cloud banks
theres a song bird flitting past
theres an itching in my fingers
for the snow is melting fast.
the water drips from twig and eaves
I ache and yawn and pine.
for a sandy beach or a grassy bank
and a rod and a hook and line.
I dont care what I fish for
the speckled trout or eel
the codfish, bass - its all the same,
oh-hum, how mean I feel.
I want to go and loaf some place
with the sun a'soaking in
a'limbering up my arms and legs
and burning thru my skin.
I want to sneak away from jobs
I want to cast a fly
I want to angle in the sea
if I dont
I know
I'll
die!

A.F. WESTERVELT

1927

"In camp, showing the two lions, Old Jack and the author after a successful day."
From "Lion Hunting in Arizona," by C.E. Ratcliffe

Outdoor Life 20¢
JANUARY 1927

Outdoor Life 20¢
JULY 1927

JUNE 1927

"A prize-winning muskellunge from practically virgin waters in Lake of the Woods."
From "The Muskellunge," by Robert Page Lincoln

When Dreams Come True

"No bull about this except the land owner's name."
From "Where the Trout Leap in Main Street," by Billie Oneal

Is She Happy? —
"Miss Anita Robinson and a catch of eastern brook and rainbow trout taken on south fork of the Santa Anna River, San Bernardino Mountains, California. Lure: pretty girl, happy smile, Royal Coachman fly."

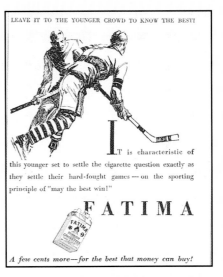

Aug. '28

COMBINED

Outdoor Life

OUTDOOR RECREATION

25 Cts.

Ozark Ripley---Hal G. Evarts---Ben Robinson---Hy Gage---Will Baird---Maurice F.

Continuing---by Ben Burbridge   TEMBO!   The Story of African Big Game

COMBINED

Outdoor Life

OUTDOOR RECREATION

Sept. 1928   Price 25¢

NEW GAME LAWS

In This Issue
C. A. Cummins---Gus Munch---Ozark Ripley---Rupert West---Harry McGuire---Col. Townsend Whelen

25 Cts.

July '28   OUTDOOR RECREATION

Hamilton Laing---Harry McGuire---Robert Page Lincoln---John Edwin Hogg---Bob Becker

TEMBO!   By Ben Burbridge---Starting This Issue

The Story of African Big Game

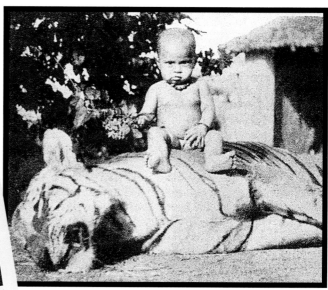

Beauty and the Beast —

"Mothers bring their babies to see these tigers in order to teach them at an early age what their greatest enemy looks like."

From "Tiger! In Hindustani: Some Encounters with the Scourge of the Jungle Deep in the Hinterland of India," by Richard Halliburton

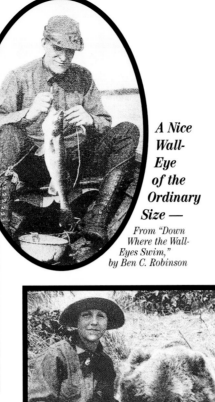

A Nice Wall-Eye of the Ordinary Size —

From "Down Where the Wall-Eyes Swim," by Ben C. Robinson

Great Bass —

Caught in Deep Lake, Florida, weighing in at 12 pounds, 4 ounces.

From "Bringing in the Fish," by H.C. Fellows

Big Game Expedition —

Mr. Slaughter, above, and the polar bear he shot on an Alaskan hunting expedition during the spring of 1927. Another member of the group, Miss Francis Ames, left, took a large brown bear.

From "Leviathans of the Arctic," by Mrs. John Borden

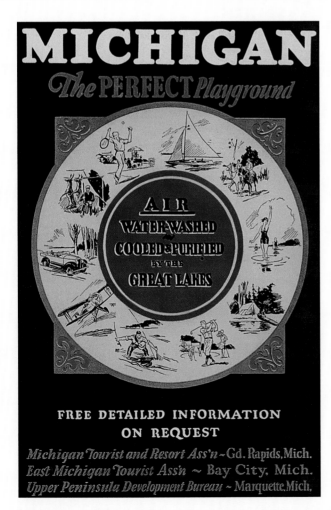
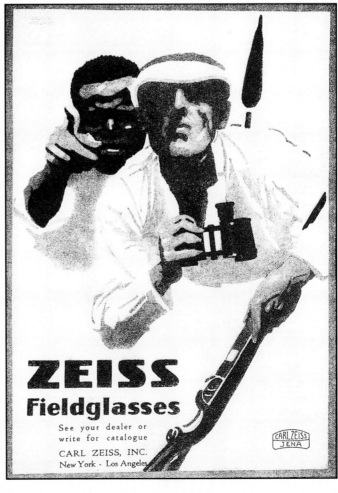

Outdoor Life

Feb. 1929 WITH WHICH IS COMBINED "OUTDOOR & RECREATION" 25¢

The Asiatic Story **BLUE TIGER** Begins This Month

A Monster Elephant of the Congo —

"I turned my glasses toward the place indicated; into them crept a line of dark objects...they were elephants...I counted about thirty, and could wait no longer; we were after them on a trot..."

From "Tembo! The Story of African Big Game," by Ben Burbridge

Outdoor Life

May 1929 WITH WHICH IS COMBINED "OUTDOOR & RECREATION" 25¢

Offering the Most Extensive WHERE-TO-GO Service Anywhere Available

"'Gators"---Archibald Rutledge

"Musky Fever"---Harvey A. Brassard

"Wading and Spinning for Small-Mouth"---Ben Robinson

Outdoor Life

Dec. 1929 WITH WHICH IS COMBINED "OUTDOOR & RECREATION" 25¢

THIS ISSUE: Wm. Barber Haynes---Robert Frothingham---Hamilton M. Laing

The Game Hog Gets His

"A nice fat black duck that came tumbling down among the decoys to pose with the hunter in this picture."

From *"My Strangest Duck Hunt,"* by William Barber Haynes

"This chap persevered until he found out about 'them moosky'."

The author fishes Lake Papoose, Wisconsin, in an effort to find out about muskies.

From *"Them Moosky,"* by Maurice Frink

"A modern Daniel [Carl Link] makes his annual examination of the residents of an alligator farm on the coast."

From *"Gators,"* by Archibald Rutledge

Sept. 1930

Outdoor Life

25¢

With which is combined
OUTDOOR ▤ RECREATION

NEW
GAME LAWS
in
THIS ISSUE

BIG GAME on ROOF of ASIA by JAMES L. CLARK

Best Of The 1930s

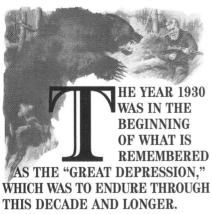

THE YEAR 1930 WAS IN THE BEGINNING OF WHAT IS REMEMBERED AS THE "GREAT DEPRESSION," WHICH WAS TO ENDURE THROUGH THIS DECADE AND LONGER.

These lean years of the 1930s dug to the bottom of most pocketbooks, crowded the unemployment rolls and generally turned the economy curve toward the depths of despair.

On the other side of the coin, the national economic disaster developed into a tremendous shot in the arm for the salvation of the nation's natural wealth.

Early in the decade, Franklin D. Roosevelt stepped into the White House as the thirty-second president of the United States. Possibly the most tremendous challenge that faced him was the rescue of the nation from total poverty and even the threat of starvation in some quarters. Most businesses were on the downhill roller coaster.

To put the brakes on this potential disaster, Roosevelt established several government-funded agencies that set up programs with jobs that were created chiefly to provide money for groceries, rent and other living essentials in average households, some of which were on the threshold of destitution.

Some of these emergency programs were designed to benefit the forests, wildlife, soil and water and other segments of our natural wealth. The Works Progress Administration (WPA) had a part in this, as did other agencies.

The big star in this sky, however, was the Civilian Conservation Corps (CCC). This agency was administered jointly by the U.S. Army, which was responsible for providing food, living quarters and medical care for the CCC workers, and the state and federal conservation agencies

that provided the work supervisors to plan and supervise the creation and establishment of new parks, forest lands, fish hatcheries and such, and to maintain those already in existence.

It wasn't planned like this, but one of the substantial contributions to our forest lands by the CCC was in the reduction of wild forest fires. Before the CC Corps was created, fire fighters had to be conscripted and often the flames destroyed hundreds or thousands of acres before the crews could be organized, equipped and transported.

The CCC work crews, which added up to approximately 200 men in each camp, were usually close enough to immediately tackle a fire caused by lightning or by a careless smoker when it was in its early stages and easily controlled, not allowed to become the kind of infernos I had fought as a forester in Montana in 1926 and 1927, with hundred-foot forest trees burning like a field of dry sedge and throwing flames hundreds of feet into the air.

Outdoor Life was one of the several nonpublic outdoor organizations that threw solid support behind the CCC programs. By written and verbal endorsement, it highly praised to its readers those public-funded activities to provide more pleasure for the outdoorsman with a rod, gun and good dog.

One of the least publicized facts about the Great Depression of the 1930s is that our game birds, animals and fish furnished an inestimable abundance of food for many families, especially in the rural sections of the nation. Being a small or tenant farmer was such a poor vocation that any income at all was barely sufficient for

essentials other than food. The CCC supervisory jobs were held by personnel with experience in their particular fields, and the workers were generally youngsters to be kept off the city streets and out of trouble.

During the early years of this decade, I was district forester for the State Forestry Department, with the eastern third of the Georgia counties, from the mountains to the sea, as my domain. My home and office were in Augusta, and all of the CCC camps involved in forestry, state parks and game lands were under my supervision. Most of my activities were centered around these conservation programs.

In 1935, I was employed as a regional forester for the National Park Service in the southeastern states, with headquarters in Atlanta. In this capacity I kept abreast of

"Behind him the fiery scavenger [the forest fire] leaves not only desolate areas and ruined forests but also the charred remains of deer and other valuable game."
From " The Trail of the Red Wolf," by Cliff Meredith

all forestry work by the National Park Service in Region One, which extended generally from Virginia to Texas.

In 1937, the Georgia legislature passed laws taking all conversation activities away from local politicians by creating a Department of Natural Resources with divisions of Forestry, Parks, Mining and Geology and Wildlife. I came back to work again with the state as first director of Georgia State Parks. A year later I was appointed commissioner of the Natural Resources Department, with the extra chore of running the Wildlife, or Game and Fish, Division.

Those were generally the conditions through the 1930s.

Outdoor Life

WITH WHICH IS COMBINED "OUTDOOR 🔄 RECREATION" 25¢

BIG GAME FISHING by ZANE GREY

Outdoor Life

August 1930

25¢

With which is combined OUTDOOR 🔄 RECREATION

The **COLLAPSE** of **CONSERVATION** in **LOUISIANA**

"Mr. Clark on his hunting yak, Pegasus, at 15,000 feet elevation in the Russian Pamirs."
From "Big Game on the Roof of Asia," by James L. Clark

O Life

25¢

Battles of the African Jungle, by W. S. Chadw

A Catch of Bass to Satisfy Any Angler —

The author, a United States Senator from Missouri, writes what he calls, "a complete treatise for both beginner and expert."

From "How to Take Bass," by Harry B. Hawes

A Killer's Last Journey —

"Yet all killers must be killed. There is not room enough on the whole earth for the white man and a single competitor; and much less room for a killer which disputes the way of the said man."

From "My Fight with a Killer," by Chas. Cottar

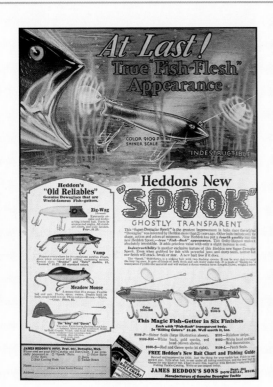

"To the trapper or hunter, poisoning of coyotes is revolting."

The author is angered by the predatory mammal control policies authorized by the Biological Survey beginning in 1916.

From "The Borgias of 1930," by Dr. A. Brazier Howell

April 1931

Outdoor Life

25¢

With which is combined
OUTDOOR AND RECREATION

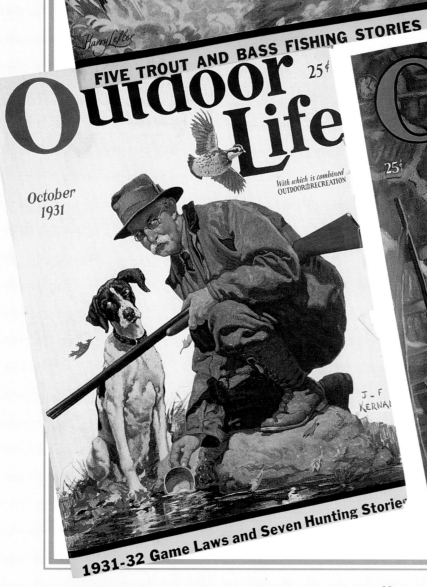

Harry Leller

FIVE TROUT AND BASS FISHING STORIES

Outdoor Life

25¢

October 1931

With which is combined
OUTDOOR AND RECREATION

J-F KERNAN

1931-32 Game Laws and Seven Hunting Stories

January 1931

Outdoor Life

25¢

With which is combined
OUTDOOR AND RECREATION

MUTTON — OR GAME? By Arthur H. Carhart

Wall-Eye —

The author and his friend Bert travel 350 miles to fish wall-eyes on Mille Lacs Lake in the wilds of Minnesota. " 'Acted like a real fish, Blackie [the author],' Bert stated, eagerly watching. 'An' there, somethin's got 'is jaws on mine too!' he decared, as he started bringing in his fish."

From "Mille Lacs Wall-Eyes," by R.M. Blackman

"The Professor, the Author and the Lawyer, from left to right, stop for a rest."
From "French River Conquests," by Ray Forbes

"H.A. Snow . . . with two wart hogs he bagged – the second being the bulgy place you observe in the python."
From "Battles of the African Jungle," by W.S. Chadwick

"What the Kodiak looks like when his huge bulk is strung up at its full length. He makes this guide look like a pigmy."
From "The Ferocity of Bears," by Stewart Edward White

1932

June 1932

Outdoor Life

25¢

December 1932

Outdoor Life

25¢ 25¢
30¢ in Canada

January 1932

Outdoor Life

25¢

Mother !!! Please wake me at 4 o'clock

CARTRIDGES

WARNER HOOPLE

A Mexican Hunting Story by Harry McGuire

Georgia Wild Turkeys —

"Ain't nothin', not even a eagle, kin see like one o' these same turkeys, yew can't bat a eyelash 'tout 'em spottin' yer."

From "Hunting Georgia Turkeys," by Morris Ackerman

"Boy! What food they afforded and how we cleaned our plates of that pink brain food fried in deep fat."

Below – A few trout with Page, Mott, and the author's father. Right – A view of the picturesque Wapiti River winding its way through the mountains.

From "On the British Columbia Summits," by Willard B. Hance

Shooting Antelopes from a Train in Colorado —

"This picture is from a sketch made near Kit Carson, Colorado, 1875. Frequently a herd of antelopes would run parallel to a train for miles, and occasionally a train would be stopped to let passengers get out and shoot."

From "Hunting in the Land of Pita," by Harry McGuire

Native Hunters and Three Moderately Large Trophies —

"They turned to see the lowered head and humped shoulders of a massive bull within 10 yards, and coming in full charge." "One was hurled aside with broken ribs piercing his lungs, as the great bosses struck him . . . another was ripped up by the massive curved horns as he started to climb a tree."

From "Killers of the Jungle," by W.S. Chadwick

1933

July 1933

Outdoor Life

25¢
30¢ in Canada

Fred Everett

February 1933

Outdoor Life

25¢
30¢ in Canada

J. Murray

Askins—Frothingham—McGuire—Gartner

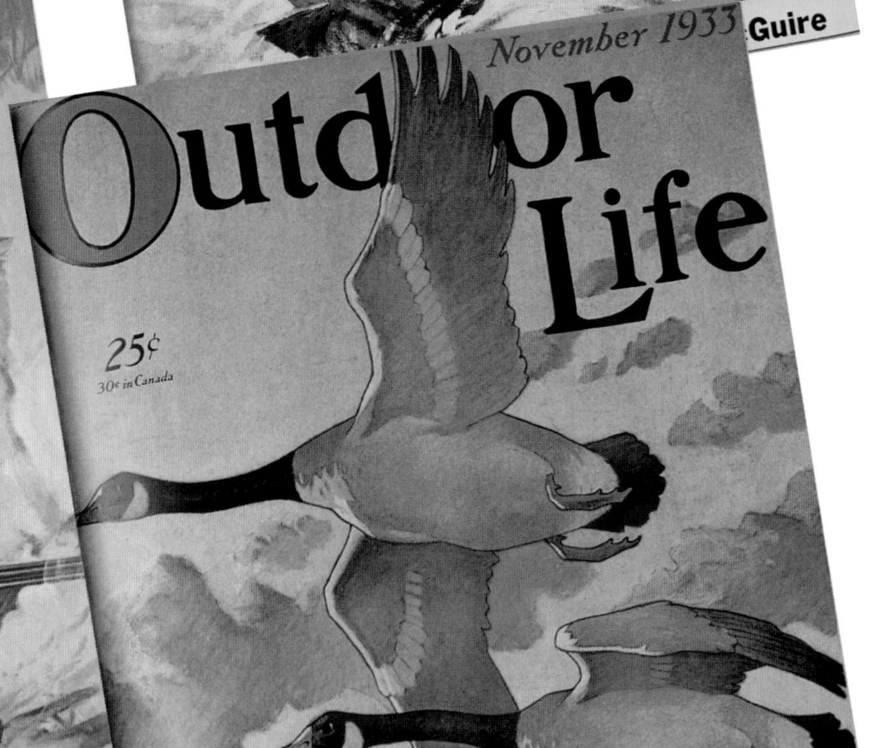

November 1933

Outdoor Life

25¢
30¢ in Canada

NRA

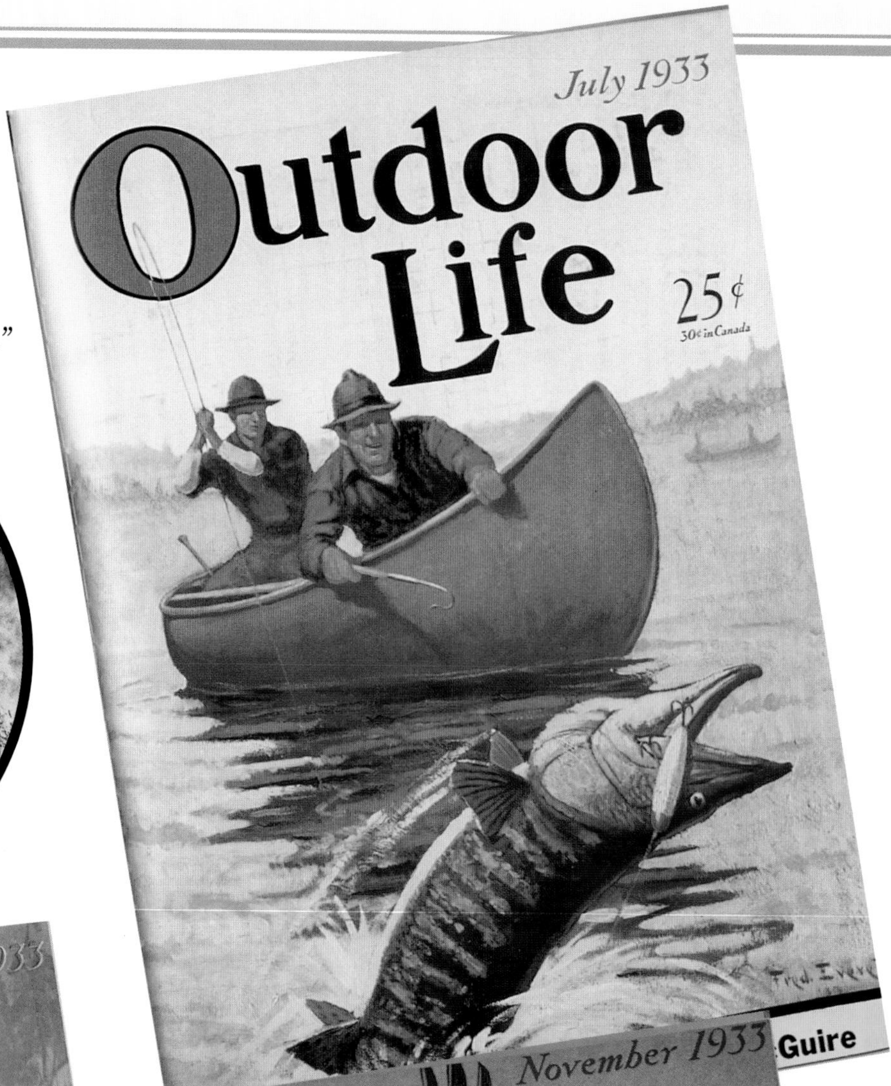

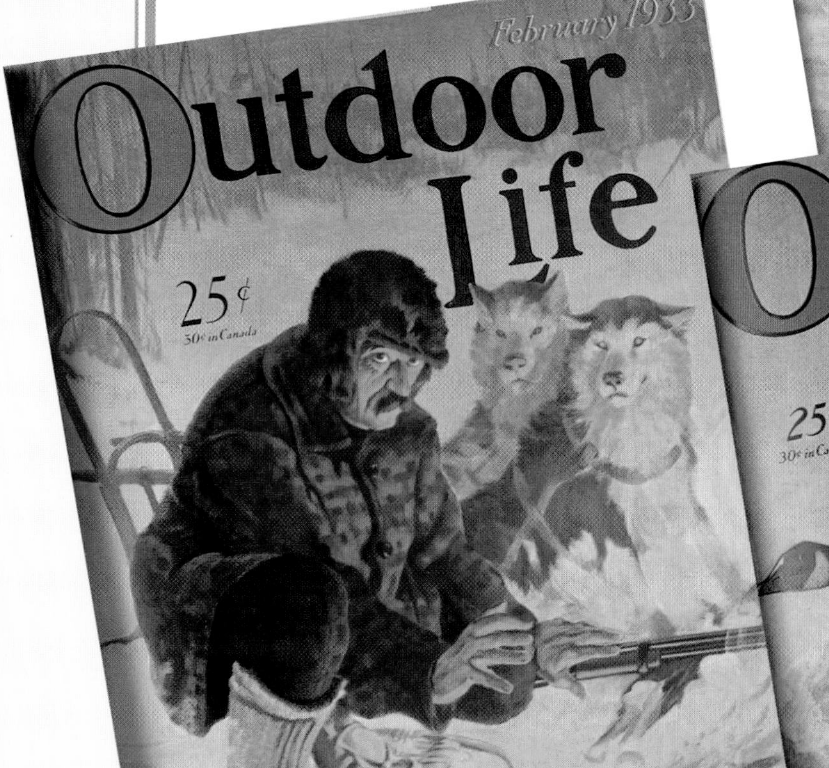

Four black bears in one hunt is the record made by Kenneth Moe, 24-year-old guide of Cloverton, Minn., according to reports received here today. The photo shows Moe beside the bears, all of which he shot in a swamp in eastern Pine county. After killing three of the bears, he had to halt to reload his rifle for the fourth, which was escaping through the dense underbrush. Several sheep have been killed by bears in Pine county recently.

Guide Bags Four Black Bears —

"Minnesota claims to be a progressive conservation state, yet it allows such slaughterers as the 'Hero' pictured here to carry stockyards standards into the hunting field. Such carnage among bears – and cubs at that! – is condemned by 99 out of 100 sportsmen, yet the sportsmen of Minnesota have not yet had the guts or the energy to get proper regulations protecting bears."

From "The 'Hero's' Corner"

Loading a Polar Bear —

The author tells of a polar bear hunt he took with his wife and two children. He had always wanted to add a polar bear skin to his trophy list, but work had kept him too busy to take an Arctic hunt. He writes, "The recent depression, however, – I trust it can be so classified by the time this story is in print – convinced me that he who does not gather roses when he may is very likely to go through life roseless . . ."

From "After Polar Bears," by Dr. Richard L. Sutton

"I believe this to be the best balanced and most graceful Stone sheep head that ever has been taken."

The author tells his story of hunting Stone sheep, nicknamed *black sheep*, north of the Peace River, in British Columbia, with his good friend, Frank Sanborn.

From "A Black Sheep Hunt . . . in British Columbia," by Jack Brewster

1934

The Truth About Wolves

By
Jack Melville

Wolf Kill —

"Most animals are cruel but few can touch the fiendishness of the wolf. He kills a great part of the time for the sport of killing."

From "The Truth About Wolves," by Jack Melville

June 1934

Outdoor Life

25¢
30c in Canada

Sutton—Rutledge—Chadwick—Everett—Barker

Outdoor Life

NOW 15¢
20 cents in Canada

FISHING · HUNTING · CAMPING · BOATS · DOGS

October

Outdoor Life

NRA CODE

NOW 15¢
20 CENTS IN CANADA

In This Issue

NEW GAME LAWS

Seasons, Limits
License Fees

Hunting the Wary Turkey Gobbler in Pennsylvania —

"America's greatest game bird, the wild turkey, now is extinct over the greater part of it's former extensive range. In only a few states is turkey hunting still worth while."

From "The Old Bronzed Men of the Hills," by Archibald Rutledge

Whitetails
IN THE LOGGING COUNTRY

"Proud to call lumberjacks their friends were these hunters during a deer hunt amid the snows of the woods."

A group of hunters travel by horse-drawn sleigh to an area near Lake Gogebic, Michigan, for a two-week deer hunt. Their efforts are rewarded with several nice bucks.

From "Whitetails in the Logging Country," by Abner Parsons

"The lists of equipment with this article were drawn up by a man with 12 yrs. experience."

From "Death Came Close to a Deer Hunt," by Major Dean Hudnutt

"A boon to the medal manufacturers; the 1933 Texas state pistol team champions."

This team, shooting individually and as a team, won more matches than any other four shooters in the history of the Texas state matches.

From "Practical Hand Gun Shooting," by Chas. Askins, Jr.

February

Outdoor Life

NOW
15¢
20 CENTS IN CANADA

FISHING · HUNTING · CAMPING · BOATS · DOGS

1935

July

Outdoor Life

NOW
15¢
20 CENTS
IN CANADA

FISHING · HUNTING · CAMPING · BOATS · DOGS

Outdoor Life

NOW
15¢
20 CENTS IN CANADA

SHING · HUNTING · CAMPING · BOATS · DOGS

NC97

GORST AIR TRANSPORT

"Casting from shore, from the wings of the moored plane, and from every vantage point conceivable, every member of the party was soon in action. With a shout of realized anticipation, one of the crowd hooked the first big trout."
From "Trout of the Skyways," by Otto M. Jones

"*Like a bolt of lightning, it came out of the tree and leaped squarely upon the spear. Five times it charged before it died.*"

Sasha Siemel has killed 125 jaguars, 27 with primitive weapons. Of the 27, he has taken 18 with his spear, 2 with bow and arrow, and 7 with a combination of rifle bayonet, bow and arrow, and spear.

From "White Spearman of the Jungle," by Tracy Lewis

"*A record kill during the past week, twenty-four deer, twenty-two antelope, nine elk, five mountain sheep and a big, silvertip bear.*"

The photo to the right shows the author demonstrating the rifle rest he used for long shots when he was a market hunter. His article chronicles the ruthless game slaughter of the 1870's.

From "Market Hunting in the '70's," by Frank H. Mayer

"*The modern boy drives a car, sails a boat, goes to movies and dances, and has a generally lively time of it. Why should he lie on his tummy and punch holes in a stupid-looking bullseye?*"

The author suggests that traditional rifle shooting matches are unpopular because they don't feature sporting rifles used under hunting conditions.

From "Is Rifle Competition Going to Seed?" by Capt. Paul A. Curtis

1936

July

Outdoor Life

NOW 15¢

FISHING · HUNTING · CAMPING · BOATS · DOGS

November

Outdoor Life

NOW 15¢

ATS · DOGS

August

Outdoor Life

NOW 15¢

FISHING · HUNTING · CAMPING · BOATS · DOGS

First Bass —

"Beside the tumbling water of a Great Smoky Mountain falls, a barefoot youngster gets his first glimpse of an older brother's native wizardry with a hand-whittled pole and worm."

At the End of the Daring Trip —

A group of men decide to try big-game fishing in the Gulf Stream, 140 miles off Barnegat Inlet, New Jersey. As the photo at left shows, they caught numbers of fine tuna on the trip.
From "New Route to Gulf Stream Fishing," by Bob Edge

"After hours of strenuous fighting, Mrs. Grinnell, tired but content, poses with her vanquished foe."

Mrs. Oliver Cromwell Grinnell was the first woman to land a swordfish with rod and reel on the Atlantic coast. She also founded the Salt Water Anglers of America, and served as its first president.
From "Lady of the Sea," by C. Blackburn Miller

Here are the QUESTIONS

upon which the anglers were asked to vote, together with a tabulation of the vote on each of the five queries:

Should any game fish, when chewed by sharks like the tuna shown below, be considered eligible for listing as a sporting record?

	NO	YES	NOT VOTING	TOTAL
1- Do you consider a mutilated fish acceptable for record purposes?	40	0	0	40
2- Does your club accept mutilated fish for record purposes?	36	0	4	40
3- Is a fish that loses its entrails considered mutilated?	19	19	2	40
4- If an angler accepts aid in bringing a fish to gaff, is the fish acceptable for records?	40	0	0	40
5- If attacked by a shark while the game fish is alongside boat, is it considered mutilated?	8	32	0	40

Members and officers of these clubs voted:

ASSOCIATED SURF ANGLING CLUBS, (Of New Jersey)
ATLANTIC TUNA CLUB, Block Island, R. I.
BEACH HAVEN TUNA CLUB, Beach Haven, N. J.
BELMAR FISHING CLUB, Belmar, N. J.
EAST END SURF FISHING CLUB, Riverhead, N. Y.
LONG KEY FISHING CLUB.
MAINE TUNA CLUB, Ogunquit, Maine.
MONTAUK YACHT CLUB, Montauk, N. Y.
SAILFISH CLUB OF FLORIDA, Palm Beach, Fla.
SALT WATER ANGLERS of AMERICA.
THE ROD and REEL CLUB, Miami Beach, Fla.
THE TUNA CLUB, Avalon, Santa Catalina Island, Cal.
VENICE—NATOMIS TARPON CLUB, Venice, Fla.

"No one can conceive of a tuna's being able to fight as hard or as well with a great chunk ripped out of it's back as he could otherwise."

The author takes a vote from members and officers of many of the most recognized fishing clubs as to whether mutilated fish should be acceptable for record purposes.
From "Keep Mutilated Fish Off Records," by Thomas Aitken

"As I began to wheel, I could just see out of the corner of my eye, a cock pheasant getting away through a fringe of naked saplings."
From "Smile When You Miss," by C. Blackburn Miller

"Many hand-gun enthusiasts and prospective shooters no doubt wonder just how the speed shot and quick draw are done, and what enables the trained gun handler to execute a split-second draw and still hit the mark."
From "Secrets of the Lightning Draw," by Barry Storm

Outdoor Life

June

Outdoor **L**ife

NOW 15¢

FISHING · HUNTING · CAMPING · BOATS · DOGS

1937

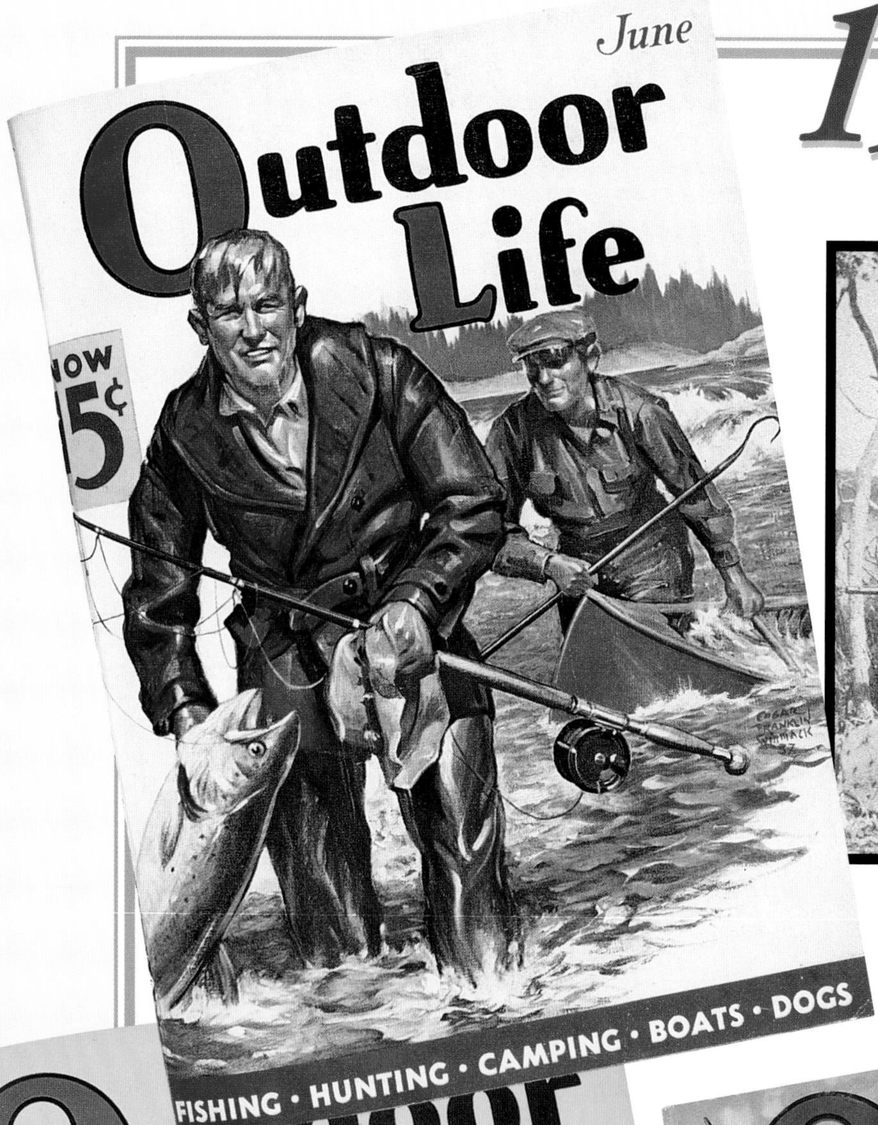

"Bush rubbed the horns together, and twisted them so that they made a sound like two deer fighting"

The author tells how he and J.L. Bushhong (Bush) learned the technique of antler rattling from a Texas game warden.

From "Rattling Antlers Gets Deer," by Fredric P. Schwab

Outdoor **L**ife

NOW 15¢

August

Outdoor **L**ife

NOW 15¢

FISHING · HUNTING · CAMPING · BOATS · DOGS

Boss of the Black Pool

"Here, in the cold depths, the Boss spent his leisure. The Black Pool was his castle. In it he lived and reigned, levying toll upon most of the living things that visited those waters."

From "Boss of the Black Pool," by Vincent Leon

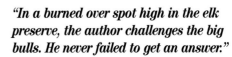
"In a burned over spot high in the elk preserve, the author challenges the big bulls. He never failed to get an answer."

The author and his friend, Charlie O'Neil, hunt elk in Selway Game Preserve, Idaho, with special licenses issued to thin the herd before winter.

From "Buglers in the Snow," by Elmer Keith

"Ready for the road. The trailer's light weight makes it easy to tow and the ample clearance permits it to be taken over the roughest trail."

From "Ideal Outdoorsman's Trailer," by Hi Sibley

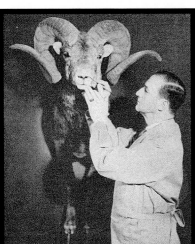

World Record Ram —

Taxidermist James L. Clark puts the finishing touches on the new world-record Stone ram taken by L.S. Chadwick. It was taken in the Muskwa River country of British Columbia. The horns measure over 50 inches in length.

From "Record on a Meat Hunt," by L.S. Chadwick as told to Walter E. Burton

First Flash Light Photo of Wild Animal —

The author writes about George Shiras III, the man who originated the sport of wildlife photography. Shiras began shooting wildlife with his 5x7-inch landscape camera in 1889 in northern Michigan.

From "The First Camera Hunter," by Arthur Grahame

August

Outdoor Life
NOW 15¢

FISHING · HUNTING · CAMPING · BOATS · DOGS

January

Outdoor Life
NOW 15¢

FISHING · HUNTING · CAMPING · BOATS · DOGS

Outdoor Life
15¢

FISHING · HUNTING · CAMPING · BOATS

Night Brings the White Bears

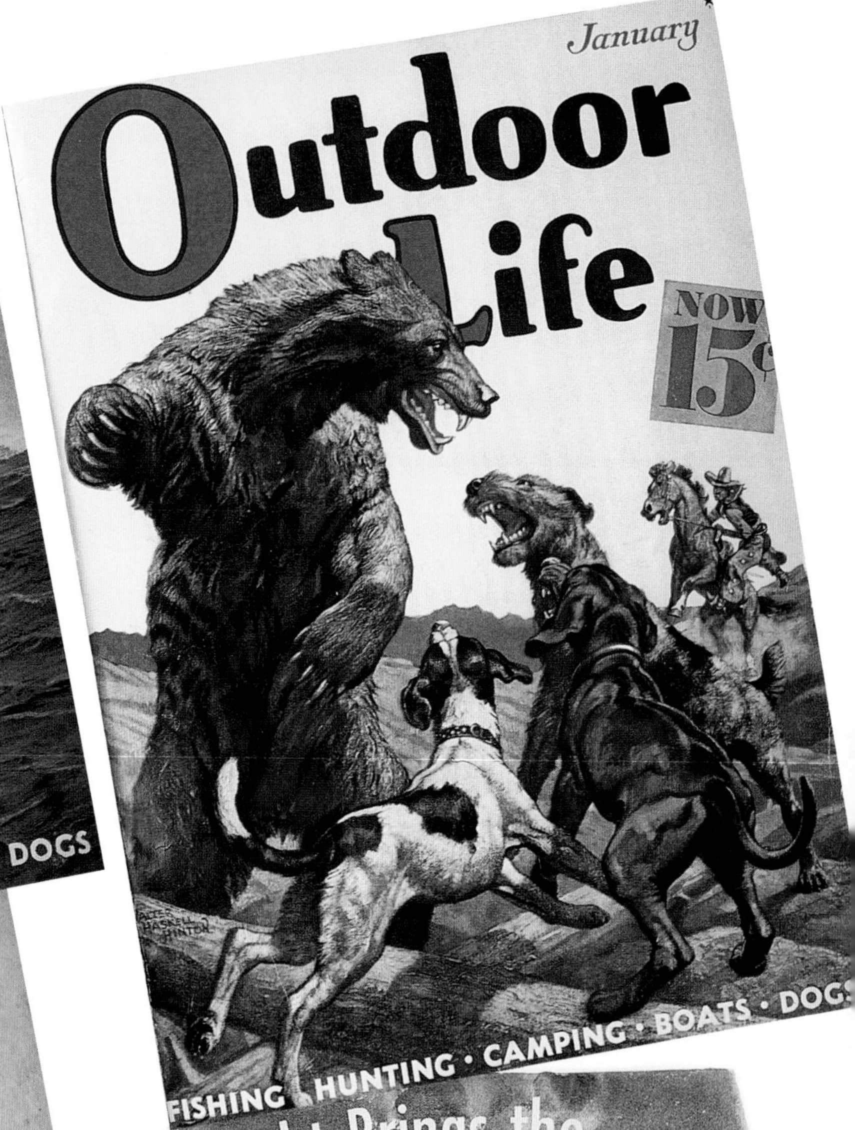

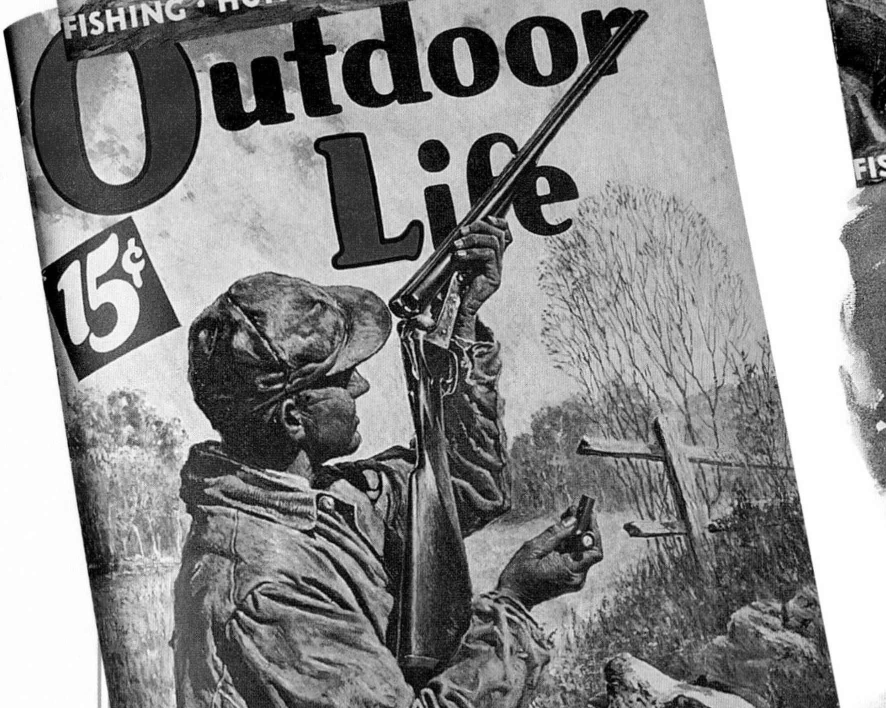

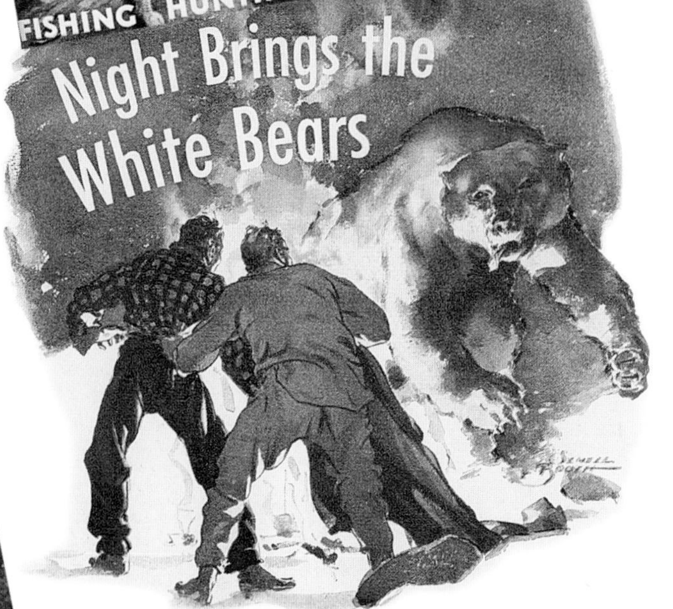

"Clad only in underwear, the archdeacon clung desperately to Jimmy's shirt tail as the polar bear chased them around the fire, red tongue lolling from his jaws."

From "Night Brings the White Bears," by Philip H. Godsell

Kaibab Muley —
In the author's opinion, the Kaibab National Forest on the north rim of the Grand Canyon is one of the finest places to hunt deer in the entire United States.
From "Grand Canyon Bucks," by Jack O'Connor

Cleaning Trout —
The author explains his unusual fishing technique: "Once the line was out, and the fly had begun to sink slowly, I took steps to time myself." "I rolled a smoke . . . when the cigarette was half-consumed, I lifted the tip of my rod, and began retrieving . . ."
From "If It's Novel, Try It on Lakers," by Nyle F. Smith

"Wearing the grin that helped make him famous, Ruth poses with the author, at left, and Jack Matthews, another hunter on the trip to the Nova Scotia woods."
The author writes of a hunt he took with Babe Ruth, who, at 43 years old, had been out of baseball for 3 years. "Just ahead of me was the Babe, walking with the characteristic little, mincing steps that all baseball fans remember."
From "Babe's in the Woods," by Bob Edge

"It may not be wise to hold up the hunt till the influence of the sun and moon is greatest, but all game is actually on the move at such a time."
From "Fish by the Sun and Moon," by John Alden Knight

NEW GAME LAWS SEASONS, LIMITS AND LICENSE FEES

Outdoor Life

September
15¢

Outdoor Life
15¢

IN THIS ISSUE:
Newest Fish & Game Laws

Outdoor Life 15¢

1939 Fishing Laws

"It would never occur to a doctor to prescribe bluegills for that tired-out feeling, but sometimes they beat any tonic you can find."
From "Fishing or Pills?" by Vic Russell

"S.E. Creasy with his pet muzzle-loader, a .65 caliber ball rifle, which weighs almost 40 pounds. With it he shot the target above."

From "Muzzle-Loaders,"
by Walter E. Burton

"Big Bill Caywood holds the rifle which time after time brought down a raging, snarling prairie gray."

The author travels 400 miles to interview history's most famous wolf killer.

From "World Champion Wolfer,"
by Arthur Hawthorne Carhart

"Suddenly I heard bones being crunched. Then, peering over the stump, I saw the killer's vague form."

The author describes killing a man-eating tiger that had terrorized natives of a village in eastern Bengal.

From "Man-Eater's Return,"
by M.A. Latif as
told to Capt.
Hugh Thomason

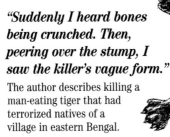

Moose Hunting —

Unimpressed with hunters who brag about shooting a moose, the author writes, "The moose is not only the frequent victim of curiosity, but at times, he displays also an indifference to danger that should have long since put him in the class with the dodo bird, were it not for the protection afforded him by man."

From "You Shot a Moose – So What?"
by C. Blackburn Miller

"Unusual rig designed to get the bait down to the big fish on the Gulf Stream's edge."

From "Going Deeper for Big Ones," by Thomas Aitken

Best Of The 1940s

THIS DECADE WAS ALMOST TWO YEARS OLD WHEN, ON DECEMBER 7, 1941, JAPAN PROJECTED THE UNITED STATES INTO WORLD WAR II BY LAUNCHING A SNEAK ATTACK THAT DESTROYED A SIZABLE PORTION OF OUR PACIFIC BATTLE FLEET ANCHORED AT PEARL HARBOR.

By enlistment and conscription, more than 16 million Americans became involved in the "war to end all wars." No computer is needed to know how vastly this depleted the ranks of men who found pleasure in hunting and fishing.

But Americans laid aside their shotguns and big-game rifles to take up the weapons of war and move all across the world. And because of *Outdoor Life* and other conservation media, those GIs who went off to fight carried with them the dreams of large-antlered bucks standing in the shadows, of bobwhites blasting out of the sedge before a steady dog, of bass or trout or tarpon in the air at the end of a line. The GIs went off to fight for those and other blessings to come home to after the job was done.

They knew their dreams of the outdoors were built on solid ground. Most of the states were now favored with stable wildlife departments, with trained personnel to enforce the regulations, do research and properly administer the units making up the department. Federal laws were on the books to provide for license fees from hunters of waterfowl and other migratory game birds, and a tax from manufacturers and dealers in hunting and fishing equipment. The millions of dollars resulting from these taxes were apportioned out to the states on the basis of the number of licenses sold. It was to be used for the improvement of game and fish resources.

The vast majority of outdoorsmen, prompted by *Outdoor Life* and other hunting and fishing magazines, and generally by the newspapers and other media, and by the manufacturers and dealers, gave their unqualified approval and support to these taxes. They endorsed the programs made possible by these funds, for game land purchase, for restocking where shootable and hookable species were at low ebb, and for the research necessary for the creation of more and better wildlife utopias.

In the early 1940s, I worked for the National Park Service as public relations director for NPS Region One, with headquarters in Richmond, Virginia. My job was to prepare news stories and edit a monthly newsletter to all employees. I came back to Georgia shortly after the state legislature created a separate Game and Fish Commission, with a commission member from each congressional district. The new commission appointed me as its director.

During this decade I wrote four books: *Conservation of American Resources*; *Careers in Forestry*; *Careers in Wildlife Management*; and *Southern Forestry*; and I rewrote *Fading Trails*, in which I was listed as "Editor." I was a regular *Outdoor Life* contributor under Ray Brown, wrote for several other outdoor magazines and published some fiction stories in the "pulps."

By 1948, Georgia had vastly increased its income from the sale of licenses and permits and was allotted sizable sums from the Pittman-Robertson and Dingel-Johnson legislation, and the smell of all this money had the politicians barking at the heels of the Game Commission. They were putting on pressure from every angle to get control of the now wealthy department and to discredit its every move.

I could envision the remainder of my public life as a continuous hassle and decided to toss in the towel and devote my time to free-lance writing. I had enough markets—and contacts.

During most of this decade I was privileged to be associated with such noted Americans of that period as "Ding" Darling; Archibald Rutledge; Nash Buckingham; and Bobby Jones, the famous golfer.

The 1940s should not be bypassed without acknowledging what Bill Rae called a "stroke of genius" by Ray Brown, who preceded Rae as editor. In 1946, Brown created and developed the *Outdoor Life* Conservation Pledge that vowed to protect and develop America's forests, soil, waters and wildlife. This pledge was immediately adopted by sportsmen's clubs, wildlife organizations, youth groups and conservationists from everywhere and became the watchword of all interested in the outdoors of our nation.

> WAR DEPARTMENT
> OFFICE OF THE CHIEF OF STAFF
> WASHINGTON
>
> Mr. Raymond J. Brown,
> Editor, Outdoor Life,
> 353 Fourth Avenue,
> New York, New York.
>
> JAN 11 1
>
> Dear Mr. Brown:
>
> I have your letter of January 8th, with inclosure, concerning the movement which you are initiating for the granting of hunting and fishing licenses without fee to members of our armed forces.
>
> The problem of providing adequate wholesome recreation for the soldier receives the constant attention of the War Department. All efforts of individuals and organizations in connection with the promotion of activities for the benefit and well-being of the personnel of the Army are solicited and encouraged. Any plan, such as yours, tending to further participation in outdoor recreational activities is considered especially desirable by the War Department.
>
> Your interest in the Army and its personnel is sincerely appreciated.
>
> Sincerely yours,
>
> Chief of Staff.

Approval from General Marshall, Chief of Staff, U.S. Army

"From every section of the land word comes in: 'Sure we'll help! Just tell us what to we can do!' Sportsmen – here's the answer."

This *Outdoor Life* editorial asks sportsmen everywhere to write to their state legislators and local newspapers calling for laws that abolish license fees for members of the armed forces.

From "The Country Speaks Up: 'Free Licenses for Service Men!'"

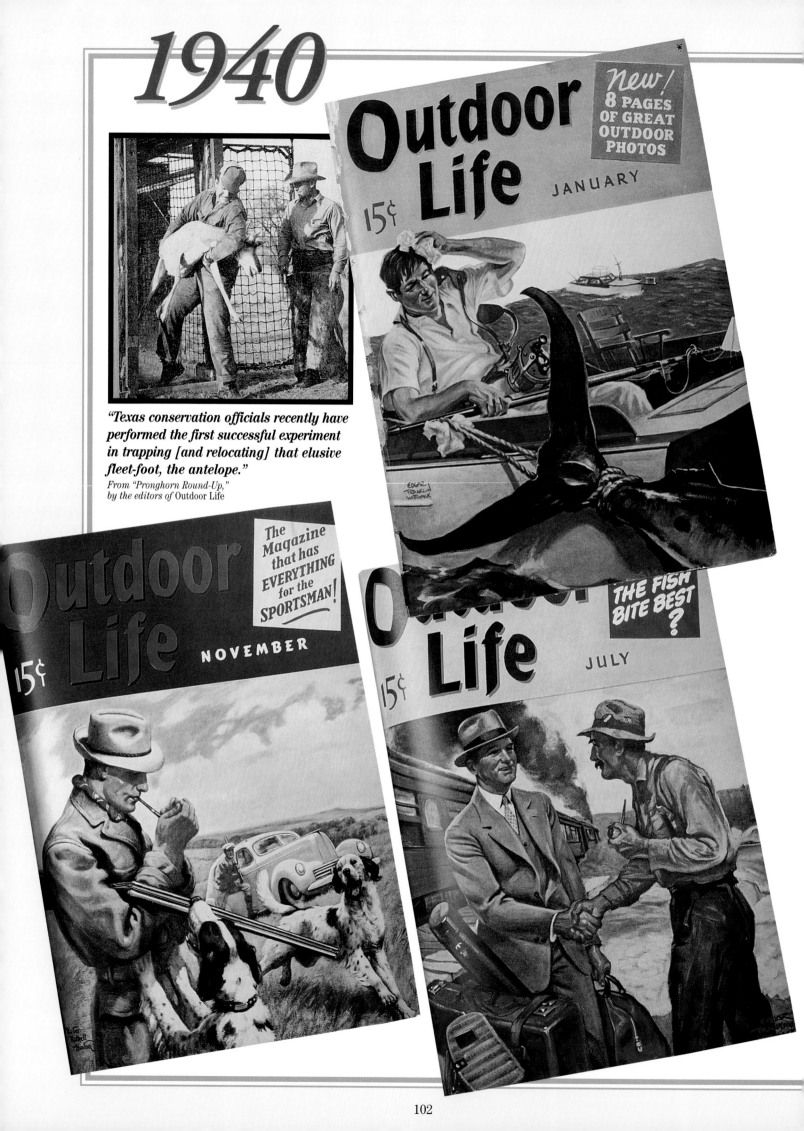

1940

Outdoor Life

New!
8 PAGES
OF GREAT
OUTDOOR
PHOTOS

15¢ JANUARY

"Texas conservation officials recently have performed the first successful experiment in trapping [and relocating] that elusive fleet-foot, the antelope."

From "Pronghorn Round-Up,"
by the editors of Outdoor Life

Outdoor Life

The Magazine that has EVERYTHING for the SPORTSMAN!

15¢ NOVEMBER

Outdoor Life

THE FISH BITE BEST?

15¢ JULY

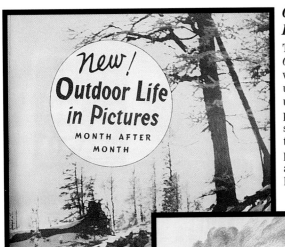

Cash For Photos —

The editors of *Outdoor Life* write, "Send us your unpublished photographs . . . so long as they're not posy or artificial-looking."

"*A fresh-killed zebra makes excellent lion and leopard bait, but it won't be good for much else afterward.*"

The author tells of an African hunt taken by ex-congressmen, B.T. Castellow, of Georgia.

From "He Found 'em Big and Tough," by Arthur Grahame

"*Some may flee, but where shall they turn for food when their forests, and yours, have been ruined?*"

From "Now It's Up to You!" by the editors of Outdoor Life

"*After a fight – and with luck – you may land [a permit]. Often, all you'll pull in will be broken line.*"

From "Gamiest Fish of the Keys," by C. Blackburn Miller

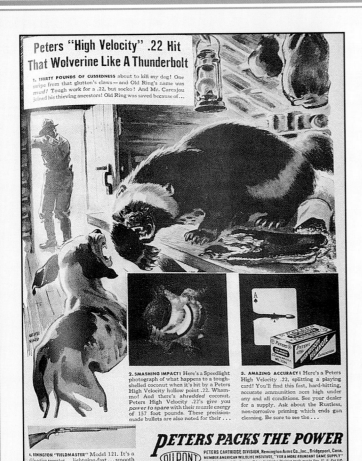

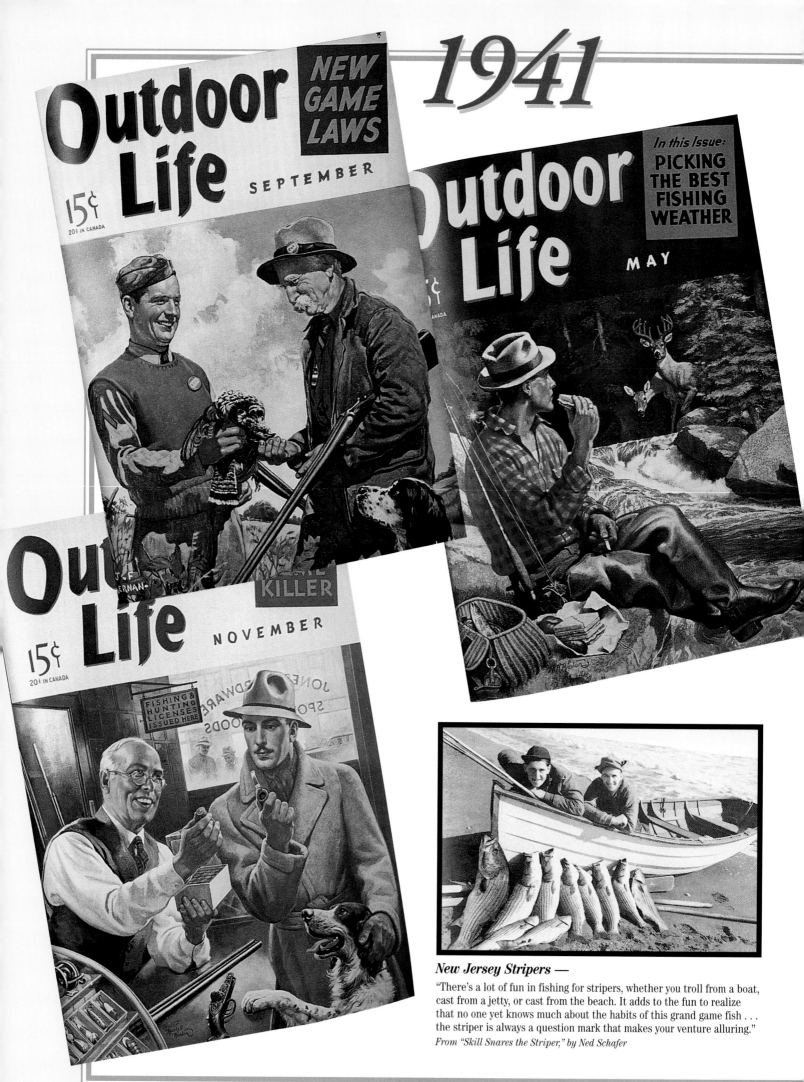

1941

Outdoor Life
NEW GAME LAWS
SEPTEMBER
15¢
20¢ IN CANADA

Outdoor Life
In this Issue: PICKING THE BEST FISHING WEATHER
MAY

Outdoor Life
NOVEMBER
15¢
20¢ IN CANADA
KILLER

FISHING & HUNTING LICENSES ISSUED HERE

New Jersey Stripers —
"There's a lot of fun in fishing for stripers, whether you troll from a boat, cast from a jetty, or cast from the beach. It adds to the fun to realize that no one yet knows much about the habits of this grand game fish . . . the striper is always a question mark that makes your venture alluring."
From "Skill Snares the Striper," by Ned Schafer

Sixguns —

The author, possibly the best pistol shot that ever lived, attempts to duplicate the shooting feats of the old-time trigger men. He writes, "I tried the famous stunt of shooting a gun out of an adversary's hand. The gun was blown to smithereens, filling the dummy's innards with bits of metal."

From "Wild West Gunmen Were Not So Hot!" by Chas. Askins, Jr.

"Well, I've been to the perfect river. I know now what it's like to find every condition perfect . . ."

The author tells of a fishing trip he took to the Serpentine River in Newfoundland for Atlantic salmon.

From "Serpentine Salmon," by Lee Wulff

"*Upland birds, ducks, geese – here's a place that has everything for the scattergun man.*"

The author writes about the annual hunt he takes to Saskatchewan toward the tail-end of September. "Each year, our Canadian shooting partner meets us on schedule, promising great things and never letting us down."

From "My Vote Is for Saskatchewan!"
by Ray P. Holland

"The freedom of the outdoors is a precious American privilege few other nations know."

From "This Is Ours to Fight For," by Logan J. Bennett

"Hauling a lusty bluegill out of a frozen lake will raise your blood pressure a few points if you've got anything in your veins thicker than rain water."

The author explains how his friend catches big bluegills on goldenrod grubs instead of mayfly nymphs, which are the traditional favorite on Wabasis Lake, Michigan.

From "Short-tailed Dinner Plates on Ice," by Ben East

Traveling Hardware Store —

"This is how I portage our power plants. 'Boy! I'd rather stay at home!' I hear you say. Well, I'll be sitting back at my ease when you are sweating over a paddle!"

From "Don't Go Light," by J.C. Hammond

"If you want to bring home some of the Yukon's best heads, just pass everything else by until they come in sight."

The author tells of traveling 4,000 miles in 15 days in order to take a guided big-game hunt in the Harris-Genere Creeks area of the Yukon.

From "Patience Pays on Big Game," by John G. Comer

1943

Outdoor Life

20¢
JULY

BUY WAR BONDS

Outdoor Life

Read: "BEAR AT BAY" in this issue

20¢
MARCH

20¢
APRIL

"My partner and I pulled our carbines from their scabbards and rode full-tilt into the mix-up."

The author writes about several encounters he's had with bears. In the scene illustrated below, the author and his partner battle three bears for over an hour in northwest Utah.

From "Danger . . . Bear Ahead," by Phil H. Moore

"The natives were ecstatic in their joy, and the welcome they prepared was fit for a Caesar."

The author tells of hunting "Old Hermit," a Cape buffalo that had brought tragedy into an African village.

From "Killers Must Die," by A.R. Siedentopf

"With a trophy like this it was easy for Jerry to forget the disappointments of two long years."

From "The Kid Gets His Buck," by Jack O'Connor

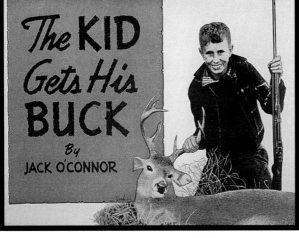

"Eight and a half pounds, and the author's pocket scales don't lie."

From "Canadian Rainbows Grow Big," by Chester Chatfield

" 'I'd rather land one of these babies,' says H.M. Stanberry, of Sisterville, W. Virginia, 'than any dozen trout or bass I ever saw.' "

From "Try Carp Just for a Change," by Ray Bergman

1944

Supporting the Fifth War Loan—15,000,000 AMERICAN SPORTSMEN

" 'America's Burma Road,' Army drivers called it. This sign post, about midway between New York and Tokyo, always gets attention."

The author, who served as a construction engineer on the Alaska Highway project, tells what to expect in the way of fishing and hunting along the 1,500-mile wilderness route when it's opened to civilians.

From "The Alaska Highway . . Sportmen's New Frontier," by R.V. Summerside

Grizzly Creek Trophy —

Arthur Henke shot this huge mule deer in 1940 near Grizzly Creek, a stream that connects to the Colorado River a few miles above Glenwood Springs, Colorado. He left the head in a gulley because it was too heavy to carry out with the meat. Later, after learning that the antlers were record-class, he returned to the gulley to retrieve the head.

From "The Head He Left Behind," by Arthur Hawthorne Carhart

"Where there are more deer on a given area than it can grow food for, there comes a day when only the hunter stands between them and a slow death."

From "Hunters: We Must Kill Off Our Surplus Deer to Save All from Starvation," by Allen Parsons

"As we carry the decoys to the beach we hear the pulse-quickening call of a mallard and, in the distance, the squeaky trumpets of geese."

From "Memo for V-Day: Pintails, Here I Come!" by Ross F. Miller

1945

"Art, left, needed husky friends to help him string up his biggest trophy, taken in 1943."

The author tells of Art Jackson, 75-year-old resident of Michigan's Dead Stream Swamp, who has killed 109 black bears.

From "109 Bears Are Enough!" by Jack Van Covering

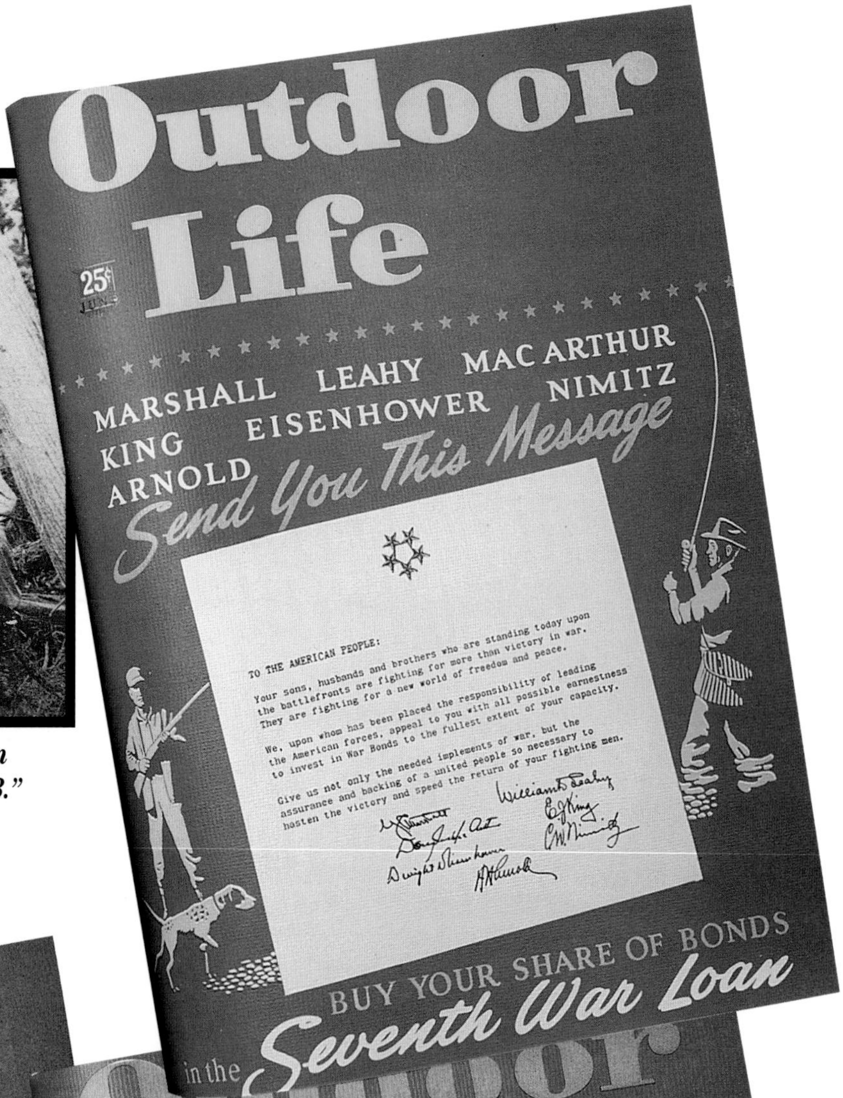

"When a 'carcass' comes to life some foolhardy hunter is likely to be hurt. Don't let it be you."
From "Be Sure Your Buck Is Dead!" by James W. Conlow

". . . the time is not far off when the manufacturers of pleasure aircraft will be pointing plenty of sales promotion in your direction."
From "Plane Talk for Sportsmen," by Henry S. Beverage

"If we want to keep on hunting, we've got to have more farmland game than ever before, because as soon as the war ends we're going to have an army of sportsmen such as this country never before has seen."
From "If You Want to Keep On Hunting . . . Team Up with the Farmer!" by Arthur Grahame

O'Connor's First Dall Sheep —

The author took his first Dall ram on a Yukon hunt near the Solomon Mountains. Hunting with Indian guide Field Johnson, O'Connor smelled the characteristic odor of a ram as they were walking behind a volcanic outcropping. At that instant, they heard rocks rolling about 175 yards above them as a big ram got up from its bed. As the animal ran full speed uphill and quartering slightly to the left, O'Connor's first shot brought the ram to its knees. The second shot sent the ram rolling a couple of hundred feet down the canyon until it came to a stop against a boulder.

From "One Whiff of Yukon Ram," by Jack O'Connor

1946

In this issue:
"TOOTSIE IS A LADY"— A GREAT DOG STORY

Outdoor Life
25¢ MAY

"Like this soldier, you can enjoy hot food despite deep snow with the Army's new midget gasoline stoves that cook with various fuels."
From "Army Gear Ready for Sportmen's Use," by Arthur Grahame

Outdoor Life
25¢ NOVEMBER
AMERICA'S PLAN TO SAVE OUR WILDLIFE

Outdoor Life
25¢ JANUARY
ARMY GEAR YOU CAN USE

Conservation Contest —

In the February 1946 issue, *Outdoor Life* announces a contest to ". . . develop a Conservation Pledge which by frequent repetition – like the Pledge of Allegiance to the Flag – will impress Americans of all ages with the urgent need for prompt united action to safeguard our soil, our forests, our waters, our minerals, and our wildlife." Rules of the contest call for an essay of not more than 1,000 words to accompany each pledge entered. There is no entry fee and you need not be a subscriber to *Outdoor Life.*

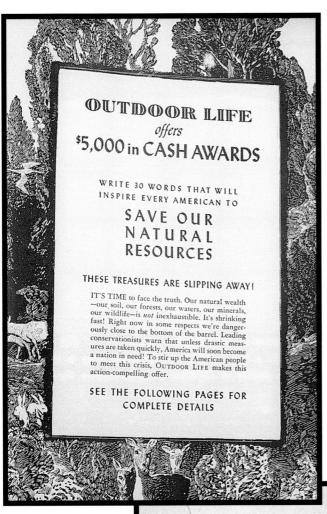

Painting Deer —

Bun Morgan is shown marking deer with an arrow that has a rubber tip, which has been dipped in thick paint. The migration patterns of the marked deer were studied to help solve the problem of game overpopulation in parts of Colorado.

From "Flying Paintbrushes Brand Deer for Study,"
by J. Martin Young

Folding Boat —

"When E. Jack Henningsen of Grand Rapids, Mich., couldn't find exactly the kind of trailer-type boat he wanted for his fishing and hunting trips, he sat down and designed his own. It proved so popular that a patent has been applied for and the craft will be produced commercially by the Michigan Twin Port-a-Boat Co. of Grand Rapids." "In addition to the plywood model shown, plastic and metal boats are planned."

From the department "Boating,"
by J.A. Emmett

"A never-to-be-forgotten spectacle – 7,000 voices make a Flint, Mich., auditorium ring to the inspiring words of America's Conservation Pledge."

All over the nation, the Conservation Pledge (shown on the January 1947 cover) has become the rallying cry for saving the country's vanishing natural treasures.

From "7,000 Adopt America's New Conservation Pledge in Record Meeting," by the editors of Outdoor Life

"As you walk along, the ruffed grouse flush up on roaring wings."

From "Wild Wings over New England: Where the Ruffed Grouse Holds His Court," by the editors of Outdoor Life.

"An instant later two big cock pheasants took off right in front of Jess and the dogs."

The author travels to California's Sacramento Valley to hunt pheasants with Jess Hogg and his well-trained pointer, Spot. But Spot is stolen just before the hunt, which causes Jess to use some of his other lesser-trained dogs. The hunt, however, goes far better than expected because the new dogs perform brilliantly.

From "A Pointer Like Spot," by Joe Mears

"Private marshes see the most shooting and the heaviest kill. The little guy gets the leavings."

From "Get Set for a Lean Duck Season," by Ben East

1948

Outdoor Life
MARCH 25¢

Outdoor Life
JANUARY 25¢
50TH Anniversary Issue

RALPH CROSBY SMITH

" 'That teensy bird?' I said.
'I don't want to shoot that!'
Wes, tight-lipped, said:
'Lady, what the hell do you
think you're here for?'"

The author writes a story of her
experiences trying to hunt with
her husband and his friends. After
a close call in which she fires "...
a few little lead pellets ..." into a
fellow hunter's leg, her husband
asks her to quit hunting before
she's sent to jail for manslaughter.

From "Guns . . . Not for Me!"
by Elizabeth Norbeck

"*A century ago it was possible for two riflemen to destroy an entire herd [of elk] without taking more than a few steps.*"
From "The Birth of Modern Firearms," by Ross C. McCluskey

"Let's raid **this** camp—they've the best of everything!"

It's a mighty thoughtful host who serves the whiskey thousands are switching to . . . mellower, milder Calvert Reserve! For Calvert's unmatched blending experience *always* rewards you with a *better tasting* drink . . . cocktail, highball or neat. Why not try it?

Clear Heads Choose **Calvert**

CALVERT RESERVE—Choice Blended Whiskey. 86.8 Proof—65% Grain Neutral Spirits. Calvert Distillers Corp., New York City

"*Barring Africa, the West of those years [1870 to 1900] was the grandest big-game country in the world.*"
From "The Golden Age of Big-Game Hunting," by Michael Norman

Merry Christmas for every smoker

Camel *Cigarettes*

Camels are *so* mild . . . and *so* full-flavored . . . they'll give real smoking pleasure to every smoker on your Christmas list. The smart, gay Christmas carton has a gift card built right in—for your personal greeting.

R. J. Reynolds Tobacco Company, Winston-Salem, N.C.

Prince Albert *Smoking Tobacco*

The colorful, Christmas-packaged one-pound tin of Prince Albert is just the gift for pipe smokers and those who roll their own cigarettes. Long known as the National Joy Smoke, Prince Albert is America's largest-selling smoking tobacco.

"*As early as 1621, settlers at Plymouth enjoyed a 'great store of wild turkeys' . . .*"
From "They HAD to Make One-shot Kills," by Fred R. Zepp

Surf Casters, NOW YOU, TOO, CAN SAY *"Goodbye to Backlash"*

IT'S HERE . . . the surf-cast model of the new Ashaway Slip-Cast Reel! All the features that have won enthusiastic praise from bait casters are now made available to the surf caster. Gives greater range to the expert . . . makes surf-casting easy for everyone . . . even the beginner.

With this remarkable new reel . . . you can make longer, more accurate casts . . . with never a fear of backlash. Reels with right hand . . . provides automatic level wind . . . fits all surf-casting rods . . . features easily adjusted drag . . . can be supplied with trigger for right or left hand casters.

the new ASHAWAY SURF SLIP-CASTER $35.00 *Federal tax included*

ASHAWAY, INC. Westerly, Rhode Island

"*Secretary of Agriculture Charles F. Brannan, left, views the Pledge with Dr. Francisco C. Banda of Ecuador.*"
From "Conservation Pledge Accepted by Congress of 21 American Nations," by the editors of Outdoor Life

Outdoor Life
MAY 25¢

1949

"Skilled hunters (right) helped open the West, but the profit-greedy killers who followed them despoiled our wildlife."

The author tells how the sale of game should have ended once the railroad caught up with the frontier.

From "How Market Hunters Massacred Our Game," by Michael Norman

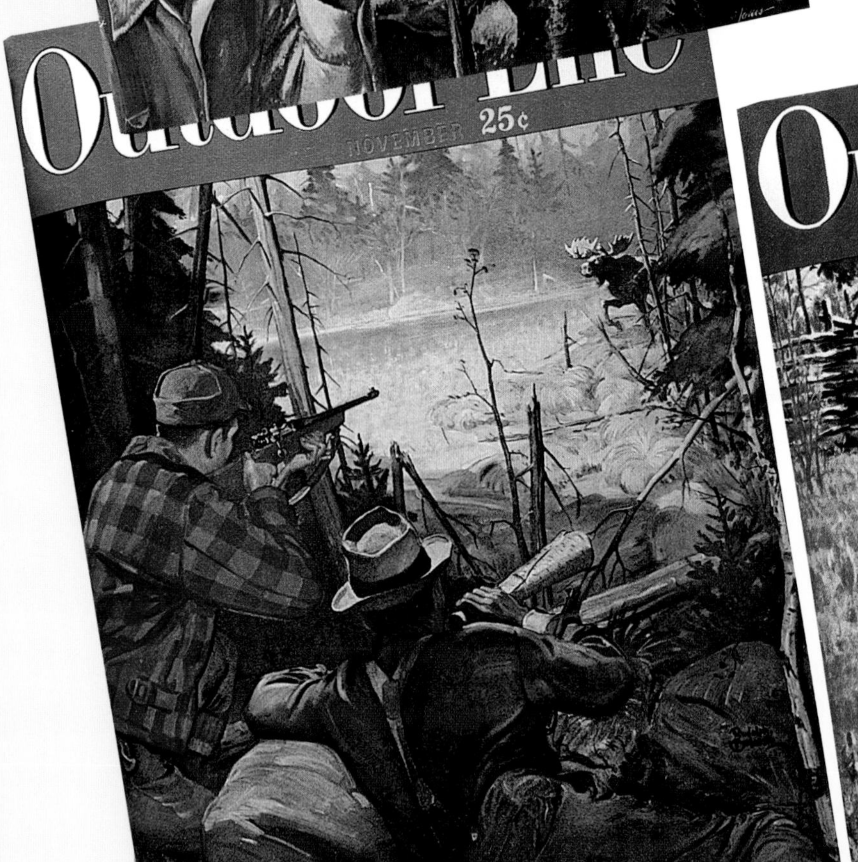

Outdoor Life
NOVEMBER 25¢

Outdoor Life
OCTOBER 25¢

"Like a coiled spring the big cat hurls his body through the air and lands squarely on his victim's back. Long claws rip bloody gashes..."
From *"Nature's Way: Cougar – Bloody Jumper,"* by the editors of Outdoor Life

"Then the coyotes close in from all sides. There may be one last, frantic dash by the quarry, but a coyote always blocks the way. Soon comes the end and the feast."
From *"Nature's Way: Death on the Plains,"* by the editors of Outdoor Life

"... like lightning his talons flashed out and struck deep into the wool of the luckless lamb."
The author witnesses an eagle attack a lamb in Clear Creek Canyon, Colorado. The eagle finally releases the lamb after a short but bloody battle with the lamb's mother.
From *"Battle of the Crags,"* by William A. Miles

"For six leg-weary hours we followed that trail blind. Then with heart-stopping suddenness it happened. In plain view were two heads right out of a deer hunter's dream."
From *"Moment to Remember,"* by S. Omar Barker

121

Outdoor Life

25¢

A PIONEER FANNIN HUNT by Jack O'Connor

Best Of The 1950s

BY 1950, WITH THE END OF WORLD WAR II SOME FIVE YEARS BEHIND IT, AMERICA WAS WELL ON ITS FEET AGAIN AND PROSPERING.

The unemployment rate was so low, the economic picture so bright and life so peaceful that we couldn't seem to tolerate it. We had to go to war with Korea and send our army of outdoorsmen to the other side of the world to fight what we termed a "police action." This went on for longer than two years, with a heartbreaking cost of more than 150,000 young Americans killed, wounded or lost in action.

I sold my first story to *Outdoor Life* when it was edited by John McGuire's son, Harry, and published in Chicago. My second feature went to Ray Brown, who took over as editor when Popular Science Publishing Co. acquired *Outdoor Life* in the mid-1930s. I was a regular contributor through the 1940s, and in 1950 joined the staff as one of three field editors.

By the 1950s, most of the states were blessed with enough federal money from such sources as Pittman-Robertson and Dingel-Johnson to acquire new areas for hunting and fishing and set up programs for more and better hunting and fishing. Funds were now available for crews to capture and restock birds and animals in those regions that had suffered from illegal or haphazard harvesting. The readers of *Outdoor Life* learned of the new methods of capture and release in the restocking programs.

One of these examples was deer. The first deer stocked were purchased and brought in from other states. Most of the whitetails stocked in my state came from North Carolina, Texas and Wisconsin. Deer from this far northern state and from the Deep South were turned into the same wooded section of Paulding County in

middle Georgia. These developed into two separate and distinct herds of Rebel and Yankee deer that seemed to avoid all contact one with the other.

The first deer for restocking were caught in camouflaged pits, but getting the animals out of those was a haphazard and rather unhealthy experience for both the biologists and the deer.

Jack Crockford, who headed the deer program and later served for years as director of the Game and Fish Division, created what he called a "capture gun." It was designed to propel a hypodermic needle loaded with a tranquilizing drug that would immobilize deer for easy handling.

The service of this "capture gun" became worldwide. It was used to transplant some huge African game animals, and even as a deterrent for very strong human criminals who had gone berserk.

A biologist in Florida told of immobilizing a very large black bear and bringing it into town where scales were large enough to weigh it.

Several very hefty farm boys ganged around the truck to see the bear. The biologist convinced them that the animal was asleep and would not waken until the effects of the drug wore off, so they agreed to help move it inside to the scales. But while the biologists were getting its weight, the bear stood up on the scales. "Those farm boys," the biologists said, "went out every door and window in the building and all at once, too." Though they immobilized the bear again, they were unable to get any help in moving it from the scales back to the truck.

When 1950 came in, the wild turkey population in the eastern states was at an all-time low. The two western species, with almost unlimited range, had fared better.

The ranges of the Eastern and Osceola (or Florida) turkeys were more confined. The Eastern bird had practically disappeared over most of its territory, from the plains to the Atlantic Ocean, and was sparsely found in only a few remaining wilderness regions, like the deep river

swamps, isolated mountain coves and on some of the southern quail plantations, where they were carefully guarded.

The 1950s was the decade in which the wild turkey began to get more attention and the first programs were organized to reestablish flocks where they no longer existed. Some of the attempts to bring back this king of game birds fell by the wayside. One was the hatchery approach, where wild eggs were hatched in incubators, the chicks brooded under artificial heat and raised on chicken feed.

Wild turkeys grown under these conditions had no chance to survive. A flock I tried to establish in a wide river swamp left the swamp to feed with the chickens on nearby farms. Those not already taken by predators ate their last meal in a farmer's backyard.

One successful method of trapping the big birds to be transplanted was to lure the birds by feeding them in a certain area, then firing a huge net out of several cannons to pin them down. This method was practically without casualties.

Outdoor Life was the first of the magazines to carry stories of this new day in turkey hunting. The wild turkey populations had come back so quickly that during the 1950s, most of the states were able to establish turkey seasons. Inspired by the stories on calling in a bearded old tom, with all of the drama involved, hunters flocking to the woods in season quickly developed turkey hunting into one of the nation's most exciting ventures in the outdoors.

"Cruising the lake in a boat equipped with an electric eye, we were able to pinpoint likely bass spots quickly."

Charles Elliott writes about fishing bass with the aid of a depth finder on Georgia's Sinclair Lake with one of his favorite angling partners, Lyman Hilliard. On this trip, Charles is in the front of the boat ready with the anchor while Lyman searches for the fishing spot by watching the red dot flashing on the depth-indicator dial in his hand. After giving Charles the O.K. to lower the anchor, Lyman says, "The way I figure it, a school of lunkers should be hovering just under that floating leaf."

"Then we'd better cast quick," Charles replies, "before it drifts out of range."

From "Depth-Finder Fishing," by Charles Elliott

Outdoor Life JANUARY 25¢

In this Issue—
6 Great Hunting Stories — including "Alaska Gave Us Everything!"

1950

Outdoor Life FEBRUARY 25¢

In this Issue—
How We Can Save The Canada Goose

Outdoor Life 25¢

" 'The kings are in!' When the word gets around, even Seattle business men find time to get out on the bay."
From "A Salmon Before Breakfast,"
by Chester Chatfield

"The kings are in!" When the word gets around, even Seattle business men find time to get out on the bay.

by
CHESTER CHATFIELD

"For Jack Frost, a rare white Siberian husky, life on the tundra was one thrilling adventure after another."

From "Snow Dog," by Frank Dufresne

"A heavily shaded pool receives its quota of [trout] fry."

From "Where They Can't Stock Fish, But Do!" by Charles C. Niehuis

"The huge fish zoomed to the surface, jumped clear, and half leaped again. Then he raced back beneath the foam."

From "Best Time for Big Pike," by Harry H. Edel

Opening Day —

Principal "Pop" Dyer (far right in photo) of Calvin Coolidge Grammar School in Shrewsbury, Mass., stops truancy on trout opener by taking all the students fishing at 4:30 a.m. The children are back in school by 8:30, with plenty of trout.

From "School's Out – for Fish!" by Frank Woolner

1951

Outdoor Life NOVEMBER **25¢**

"My hand and half my arm were in the shark's mouth before either of us was aware of it."
From "Eight of My Lives," by Archibald Rutledge

by John Durant

Outdoor Life DECEMBER **25¢**

THE MOST DANGEROUS HUNT of ALL by Berry Brooks

Outdoor Life MARCH **25¢**

In 5 Days
WE SHOT
THE WORKS
Elk, Goats, and a
Grizzly!...PAGE 46

"Snap the prongs together, twist them apart, and be ready for action. A buck may turn out ready to do battle with man or beast."

The author writes about how the technique of rattling was invented in the mesquite-and-cactus country of Texas. He says, however, that rattling works in every state where the deer season coincides with the rut.

From "Why Not Try to Rattle Up a Buck?" by Hart Stilwell

"I dared not chance a shot, for the bobcat and the dog were a pinwheel of snapping, snarling, ripping fury."

From "This Bobcat Needed a Lesson," by Carl T. Johnson

"If he manages to run down a man, he'll toss his victim into the air with a sweep of his sharp front horn, or crush him to death beneath massive feet."

This painting is the ninth in a wildlife series by Bob Kuhn, who was commissioned by *Outdoor Life* to depict – in full color – the world's largest game animals in their native habitats.

From "History's Ugly Hangover . . . The Rhinoceros," by the editors of Outdoor Life

Outdoor Life 25¢ FEBRUARY

Outdoor Life 25¢ DECEMBER

No Job too BIG for Sam

How to scare up TOO MANY LIONS by Ralph Hammer 25¢

...SE OF THE WITEGOO, a wilderness quest for trout.

ROY CHAPMAN ANDREWS REPORTS A RARE HUNT...

North Korea Ducks —

The author writes, "The scene is Wonsan Harbor, North Korea; the time, January, 1952; my weapon, a bolt-action Springfield of vintage 1918; my duckboat, one of Uncle Sam's 2,100-ton destroyers. The box score: eleven ducks (Communist, of course), eight on the wing and three sitting."

From "Wonsan Incident," by D.J. Carrison

"Hunt a wild boar with hatred and shoot him with bloodthirstiness." "What he will do to the bravest dogs in the world will make you lust for his death."

From "In a Pig's Eye," by Emmett Gowen

No. 1 Alaska Moose —

The author is shown measuring the new world-record Alaska moose. It is 1 of 24 new entries in the latest edition of *Records of North American Big Game.*

From "24 New World Records," by Grancel Fitz

"WAAH, I WANNA HOLD HIM!"

Three-year-old Stanley James (left), who has a broken arm, feels left out when his sister doesn't let him hold a fish she's caught.

From "For to Catch a Whale," by Helen M. Wells

Outdoor Life JANUARY 25¢

1953

VINTER HUNT, two miles up in a blizzard p. 17

Outdoor Life AUGUST 25¢

RICK UP YOUR CASTS P. 30—END OF THE EARTH P. 52

Out

"No merlins for Jule Mannix. She hunts iguanas with Aguila, a 12-pound bald eagle."

From "For the Girls: Lady Falconer,"
by Elizabeth Norbeck

rculation Of This Issue Over 1.000.000

Greater Kudu —

The author once rated the lion, the elephant, the rhinoceros, and the buffalo as Africa's finest trophies. But he now feels that the greater kudu is the top prize. He writes, "Of all the animals I have hunted, I believe he is the most restless, the most suspicious, the best able to thwart the hunter. Going after the kudu combines the toughest features of hunting mountain sheep and stalking whitetail deer."

From "Africa's Top Trophy,"
by Jack O'Connor

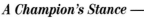

A Champion's Stance —

Gloria Jacobs Norton began shooting handguns competitively at age 12. Now 30, she holds 12 of the 15 recognized women's records.

From "The Lady Is a Champ," by the editors of Outdoor Life

Monster Brownie —

Melville N. Lincoln (left) is chief curator for the Los Angeles County Museum. H.T. Beck (on ladder) is the museum's taxidermist. The two men and J.R. Sewell, the staff habitat-background artist, were on a research trip to Kodiak Island, Alaska, to observe the region so the museum's new bear display would be completely realistic. Rather unexpectedly, the men were charged by a huge brown bear, which was shot by Roy Lindsley. The bear's skull measured $17^{15}/_{16}$ inches long and $12^{13}/_{16}$ wide.

From "World's Biggest Bear,"
by Ed Ainsworth

1954

Outdoor Life SEPTEMBER 25¢

The Art
of Sheep Hunting
by
Jack O'Connor

Late-Season Fishing

Outdoor Life AUGUST 25¢

HOW TO CATCH
BASS IN AUGUST

NEW WAY TO FISH p. 25 – ESCAPE FROM ICY DEATH p. 50

Outdoor Life 25¢

THE LOST HERD p. 29 – HOW TO SOUND OUT DEER

SPRING FISHING SPECIAL ■ MY MOST DANGEROUS HUNT p. 41

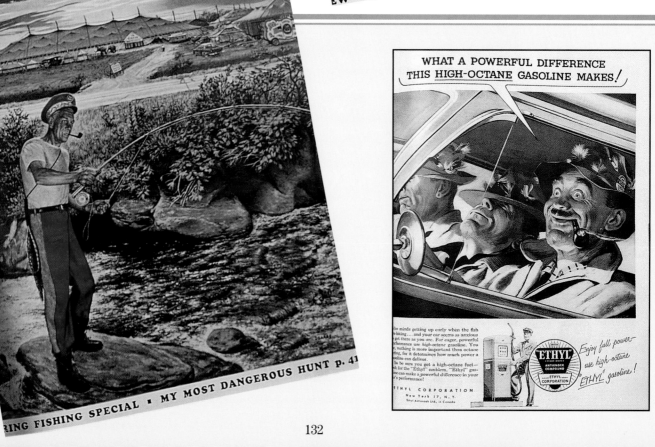

"The black wolf jumped for Punyuk's shoulder as the Eskimo struggled to his feet, his scalp and leg already torn and bleeding."
From "Will Wolves Attack a Man?" by Frank Glaser as told to Jim Rearden

Bowhunting New York —
The author (left) describes one of the first deer seasons held in New York's Washington County. He hunts with his 16-year-old son, Allan, and Adirondack woodsman Okey Butcher, who is shown (below) pulling arrows from a straw target that has a deer tail attached. The author, hunting from the ground, shoots a small buck with a 20-yard shot.
From "We All Wore Green," by Lee Wulff

Muzzle-loaders Only —
T.C. Robinson, 70, aims in the annual Cataloochee Beef Shoot in North Carolina's Great Smoky Mountains. Prizes are quarters of beef for men, a cigarette lighter for the leading lady.
From "Beef Shoot," by the editors of Outdoor Life

1955

Rare Sheep —

The author writes about how British Columbia is relocating some of its California bighorn sheep to Hart Mountain National Refuge in Oregon. The sheep, which number less than 1,000 in the province, have little chance to survive because ranchers in central British Columbia have taken over the bottom lands that were once the sheep's winter range.

From "Moving Day," by Bill Thomas

Outdoor Life JANUARY 25¢

Read What Happens
...m 350 African Buffalo
...rge 3 Men and A Boy

Charles Dye

NEW WAY TO HUNT: WE DRIVE OUR OWN 12-BED VAN p. 21

Outdoor Life DECEMBER 25¢

2 Mi.
CHINOOK
PASS
ELE. 11,124

LOW
SLOW
GEAR

...light of Cruel Cold p. 32 — New York's Big Bear p. 46

Out...

HOW TO CATCH YOUR FAVORITE FISH

...SHERMEN'S FEUD — WALKED TO DEATH — WEEK IN THE WILDS

*"He was one big tiger –
the biggest I've ever seen a
picture of."*
From *"O'Connor in India: A Tiger Has Killed,"*
by Jack O'Connor

Fox Calling —

The author (left) tells about the first time he tried fox calling. He writes, "So I squealed like a rabbit and squeaked like a mouse – and along came Red."

From *"The Squealer,"*
by Frank Heidelbauer
as told to Ben East

The Muskie Rampage —

The photo below shows muskies hanging like sides of beef at Federal Dam, Leech Lake, Minnesota. In mid-July, 105 muskies are caught in a five-day period.

From *"Five Crazy Days,"*
by Jack O'Connor

7-pound 'bow —

Bebe Anchorena (above) holds a big rainbow trout taken from the Chimehuin in Argentina.

From *"The Hat Trick,"*
by Joe Brooks

APRIL
Outdoor Life 25¢

Charles Dye

Fishing's Big News p. 54

Calendar for Trout p. 64

Best Place to Hunt p. 68

New Fishing Laws p. 24 — O'Connor's Persian Boar p. 62

OCTOBER 1956 35c
Outdoor Life

CONQUERED!
River of No Return
see Page 72

JOHN FLOHERTY JR

mart Deer — East or West? p. 64 — New World Record p. 6

Outdoor Life 25¢

Geoffrey Biggs

O'Connor in Iran p. 33

I Shoot A Record Moose p. 36

Great New Gamefish p. 38

Fishing's Hottest Secret p. 60

XTRA: 30-Page Section on New Boats and Motors

"Russ Cowger, Bob Ellis, and I, left to right, at weighing-in of my Clover Pass [Alaska] catch – 42½ pounds."

The author writes about fishing Alaska for king salmon: "I met the mighty chinook in both his realms – rivers and the sea – and found him all a monarch should be."

From "The King and I," by Grancel Fitz

" *Everybody in Healy, Alaska, came out to see the sea of caribou. Two fellows disarmed the one gun-toter.* "
From "The Crazy Deer," by Frank Glaser as told to Jim Rearden

"*It's Alaska's Brooks Range – huge, remote, unexploited. We shot caribou, sheep, bear; saw big-game herds eye us unafraid. You too can go there by plane.*"
From "Best Place to Hunt," by Jim Rearden

"*The author swings for easier going-away shot at dove zipping over his Joshua-tree blind.*"
From "Spots Before My Eyes," by Joe Mears

"*Agent Frank Clarkson with illegal waterfowl found in raid.*"

This article details the work of U.S. Fish and Wildlife Service undercover agents and their assignment to break the outlaw ring of waterfowl bootleggers in Texas.

From "Texas Man Trap," by Bob Brister and Ben East

1957

35¢ · OCTOBER, 1957

Outdoor Life

REVOLUTIONARY NEW TRAP
How It Works
page 71

NEW WORLD RECORD RAM
Story on page 56

FEBRUARY 1957

Out

Thrilling Grizzly Bear Photos page 53 / World's Best Bass Lake page 60

In This Issue

I FACED TOO MANY BEARS
· · ·
CAN YOU OUTWALK A DEER?

SPECIAL: 26-Page Section on New Boats and Motors

"Erickson [standing] and helpers watch as ether wears off and bear recovers senses. Bears react unpredictably during this ticklish period."

The author catches a Michigan black bear in a live trap as part of his wildlife research aimed at solving a few of the riddles in the life history of the animals.

From "We Tag Live Bears," by Al Erickson

35¢ · JULY, 1957

Outdoor Life

Boom in Sports Trailers:
What to look for in a camp on wheels
page 32

The Grayling page 56

ive Best Bets for Bass page 25 | We Put Tags on Live Bears page 38

138

" . . . there wasn't any way I could stop sliding down toward that cat. All I could do was shoot in her ear as I jumped over her."

From "Lion in My Lap," by T.J. (Shorty) Lyon

Cuba Bass —

Georgia Tech's head football coach Bobby Dodd holds a nice bass caught from the fabulous Zapata swamp of Cuba.

From "Best Bass Lake on Earth," by Charles Elliott

10-foot Cougar —

The author is shown with his Montana cougar. Its skull measured $\frac{1}{16}$ inch shorter than Teddy Roosevelt's world record cat from 1901.

From "Biggest in 52 Years," by Lowell S. Hayes

"Trout in tiny pool will see angler at left. Since fish is facing into current, man at right's less likely to spook it."

From "Pocket Fishing," by Howard T. Walden II

1958

Outdoor Life
35¢ · DECEMBER, 1958

How Agent Trapped 94 Market Hunters

How to Find Bass

O'CONNOR IN AFRICA
World Record LEOPARD

BONUS HANDBOOK How to Buy Rifle Accessories

Outdoor Life
35¢ · JUNE, 1958

Tricks for Big Trout by Joe Brooks p. 33

How to Go Camping on Vacation p. 60

HOW TO FISH FROM SHORE p. 46

TIPS ON HUNTING WITH A CAMERA p. 36

Outdoor Life

O'Connor in Africa

How to Buy A Hunting Dog

Do Brown Bears Attack? SEE PG. 41

The Betty O —

For a decade the runs of 30- to 50-pound white sea bass had tapered off along the shores of Southern California, but word was out that the big whites had returned. The author writes, "The Betty O is a clean, wide-beamed, 65-footer that's ideal for live-bait [squid] party fishing. Along with another boat, the Dinah Lee, she makes daily runs out of the cove. Fares are $6 for an all-day trip, $3.50 for a half-day trip."

From "Big Whites Return," by Lupi Saldana

CK O'CONNOR IN AFRICA:

Outdoor Life
OCTOBER 1958

"O'Connor and Geraan guide with white oryx taken on fringe of the Sahara, about 1,500 miles from conventional safari country."

From "We Hunt Rare Sahara Game," by Jack O'Connor

"Walt hefts our string of shad-chasing bass."

The author and his Louisiana guide, Walt, catch black bass that are chasing shad on the surface. They catch the fish on topwater lures and deep-running wobbling plugs.

From "New Bass Strategy," by Hart Stilwell

"Charlie casts a new fly pattern while Vince observes reaction of feeding trout. This unique team approach solved many problems."

From "Jassids – New Approach to Fly Fishing," by Joe Brooks

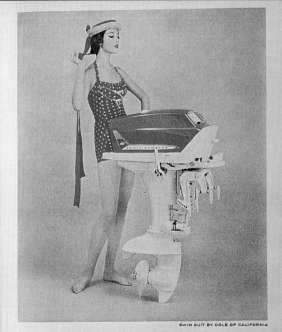

1959

"Like a line of medieval lancers awaiting enemy charge, fishermen brace against oncoming breaker laden with smelt . . ."

From "Big Scoop," by Darrell F. Brown

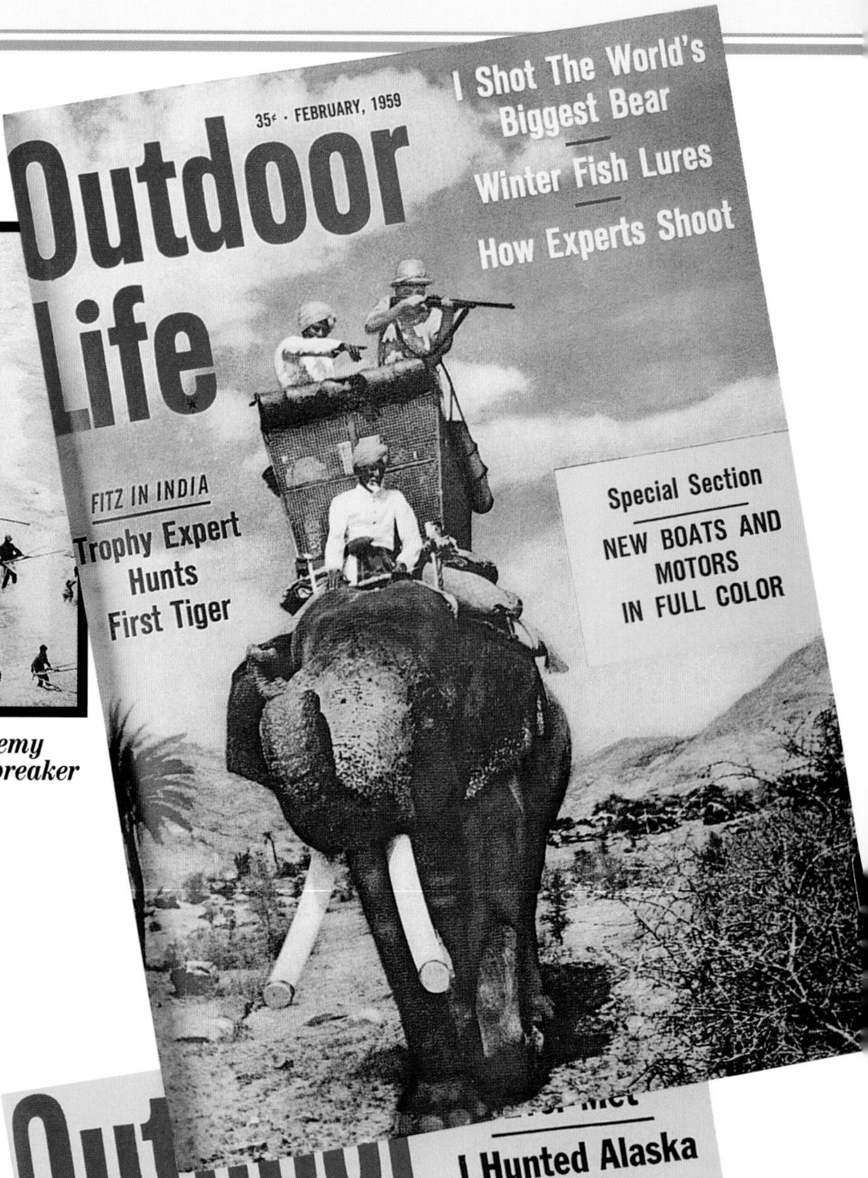

35¢ · FEBRUARY, 1959

Outdoor Life

I Shot The World's Biggest Bear

Winter Fish Lures

How Experts Shoot

FITZ IN INDIA
Trophy Expert Hunts First Tiger

Special Section
NEW BOATS AND MOTORS IN FULL COLOR

35¢ · JULY, 1959

Outdoor Life

$50 Wilderness Vacation

Great New Fishing Country

Camera Shows How JOE BROOKS PLAYS AND LANDS FISH

The Big Muskie Myth

Outdoor Life

I Hunted Alaska Alone

Now Every Month ARCHERY

HOW I BAGGED Three World Records ON ONE HUNT

Christmas Trout

"Catching a fish in this crowd was a community affair."

The author describes fishing for kokanee on Lake Stevens, Washington.

From "The Uncatchable Kokanee," by Chester Chatfield

"Even in country where the mountain lion is common, it is very rare that one is seen unless it's put up a tree or otherwise bayed by dogs."

From "The Mountain Lion," by Jack O'Connor

South Dakota Pheasants —

The author writes, "Pheasants are running even more than they used to, but there are ways to get them aloft. Here are some."

From "Ringneck Runaround," by Ben East

35¢ · APRIL, 1960

Outdoor Life

10 SECRETS FOR CATCHING TROUT

BIGGEST NEWS ON WHEELS

Mobile Sport Camps

New Fishing Laws

Best Shot 'll Ever Make

W·R·

Best Of The 1960s

JOHN FITZGERALD KENNEDY WAS ELECTED THIRTY-FIFTH PRESIDENT OF THE UNITED STATES IN 1960.

Sentiment was either very favorable or very critical of many of his actions, such as our Bay of Pigs invasion of Cuba, the escalation of the war in Vietnam, the improvement of our space program and the establishment of the Peace Corps. But all of these were put on the back burner as Americans were stunned by the assassination of President Kennedy in November 1963 in Dallas, Texas.

In February 1957 and in the last issues before this decade began, *Outdoor Life* introduced a new feature— "Reports from the Field"— to cover all happenings that affected the hunter, fisherman and outdoorsman. This news was prepared by the field editors and others on the staff; its purpose was to bring the reader up-to-date on conservation events of interest and on local and national changes that in any way affected hunting or fishing.

In April 1961, the title of this feature was changed to "Roundup" and carried more general news, with items submitted by the readers. These pages proved such a popular feature that by October 1968, to use all the news flowing in from many of the nation's outdoor columnists and from the readers, *Outdoor Life* expanded from one national issue into four regional issues, with each regional carrying its own yellow pages filled with news of happenings in that section of the country. Except for this regional feature, the excellent hunting, fishing and adventure stories by the top word craftsmen were the same in all issues of the magazine.

One of the vital criteria under the editorship of William E. Rae, who served as editor from 1951 until 1973, was that all stories must be true and accurate accounts of actual experiences with a rod, gun or other outdoor gear. Any writing that smelled like fiction was absolutely taboo.

During Bill Rae's guidance, one tradition for which *Outdoor Life* was especially noted was closely followed. This was the policy of helping any writer of a story that had the possibility of publication. The editors made suggestions to improve

"Bergman in brook-trout country – Ecorces Lake in Quebec, Canada."

In 1960, after 26 years of writing the angling column for *Outdoor Life*, Ray Bergman delivers his final message: "I am going to fish for a while in a lazy, indolent way without writing about it. Farewell for the present. I wish you all good health, long life, and many tight lines."

From "Ray Bergman Says Goodbye," by Ray Bergman

the writing or the story line. Often, when an author with an exciting experience was unable to tell it properly, the rewriting was assigned to a member of the editorial staff. Usually a story could be rewritten from the submitted version, but occasionally a visit and interview with the original author was necessary. Some of these rewrite jobs proved more interesting than the story originally submitted by the author.

One I vividly remember was the account of a trip down Daddy's Creek in east Tennessee. The story line was a fishing trip for muskies planted in those waters.

Very briefly, the theme concerned a float trip of six or eight hours from one bridge to the next below it, where we would be met at the end of the day. We didn't float that canyon in eight hours. We were there for three days, pulling our boat over barriers of jagged slabs of stone where the creek flowed under walls of rock that had broken off the canyon walls. We dragged the boat over inch-deep shoals of granite farther than we paddled it. No muskies. The few small bass we caught kept us from starving. My companion finally admitted that his story was about a trip he had made down the canyon twenty-five years before, when the stream was open all the way.

In this instance I gave his story back to him and wrote one of my own.

Another story turned over to me for rewriting was from the typewriter of a well-known sports editor with a nationally syndicated column. His forte was organized sports and, as far as I knew, he never wrote any outdoor copy. His facts were excellent but not passed on in the proper language for outdoor telling. It was about a fishing experience with an equally famous sports personality. The pictures to illustrate the story were made by the newspaper staff photographer and were excellent.

So I rewrote the story and *Outdoor Life* paid the newspaperman a handsome check and gave his story a prominent spot in the magazine.

I assume that my sports editor friend was irritated to have his deathless prose rewritten by a lowly field editor. He didn't speak to me again for two years.

1960

35¢ • JANUARY, 1960

Outdoor Life

We Hunt Meanest Bear

I Shot Biggest Elk of the Century

40 Sleeps North

A Wild Fishing Adventure

Cover Story on Pg. 33

35¢ • OCTOBER, 1960

utdoor fe

Discovered A New World of Hunting
by Grancel Fitz

Hunting HERE

Most Dangerous Game?
THE BROWN BEAR
by Jack O'Connor

50 Experts tell you **WHERE TO GET DEER**

Outdoor Life

Finally Gets Leopard

Bird Nobody Can Hit

This Happened to Me! Pg. 64

BOUNTY HOAX
$1,000,000 Throwaway

New Varmint

Deep-Sea Mystery

Falcon Lake, Mexico —

The author and Dave Hawk (above) fish largemouth bass among the ruins of Old Guerrero, a town flooded by Falcon Lake when the Falcon Dam was built across the Rio Grande River.
From "Fishing Down Main Street," by L.A. Wilke

"Ralph Gray with his 68½-pound striper. Only 1½ pounds lighter than the world record."

From "Day of the Monster," by Frank Woolner

Stray Muley —

This mule deer strayed into downtown Minneapolis, Minn., was struck by a car and suffered a broken leg. The deer was then tied to a traffic meter while an officer made his report. A local game warden later found it necessary to kill the deer because of its injuries.

From the column, "What's on Your Mind?"

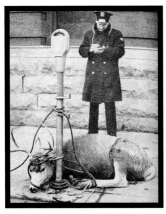

"I was gasping for breath, and I knew the shot was impossible. But my guide said, 'Shoot! Quick!', and I let fly instantly."

Fred Bear tells of becoming the first white man to take a Stone ram with bow and arrow. Hunting in northern British Columbia with Indian guide Charles Quock, Fred misses his first shot at a huge ram. They pursue it for several hours until Fred gets another chance. This time, however, only the ram's head is visible over the ridge at a distance of 40 yards. In a split second, Fred draws his bow "short," then lobs the arrow over the ridge so it drops below the line of sight and into the ram's brisket.

From "Best Shot I'll Ever Make," by Fred Bear as told to Bryon W. Dalrymple

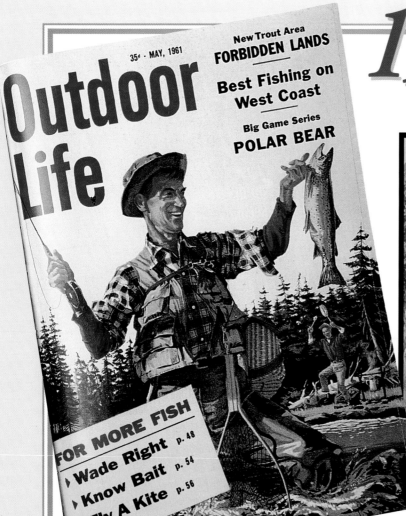

1961

Outdoor Life — 35¢ · MAY, 1961

New Trout Area
FORBIDDEN LANDS

Best Fishing on West Coast

Big Game Series
POLAR BEAR

FOR MORE FISH
▶ Wade Right p. 48
▶ Know Bait p. 54
▶ Fly A Kite p. 56

Pointer —
"Hard working, rangy, he dominates pointing-dog trials. He's an inch or so higher at the shoulder than an ordinary English setter and weighs about the same."

From "A Gallery of Hunting Dogs: Four Great Breeds," by David Michael Duffey

Outdoor Life

Most Honest Record
THE 41st BEAR

SHOTGUN TRAINING
An Admiral's Secret

New Hunting Laws

Why Pheasants Are Foozled

"Best Deer Country Anywhere" —BUCKSKIN BONANZA

SPINNING'S LATEST THRILL

Outdoor Life — OCTOBER, 1961 · THIS ISSUE **35¢**

Biggest Ever
SPECIAL HUNTING ISSUE

BONUS "PULLOUT"
4 paintings to frame

BEST HUNTS THIS FALL
a nation-wide survey

GUNS YOU NEED
for all kinds of game

EXPERTS TELL YOU
▶ What to wear
▶ How to shoot
▶ Where to go

HOW TO DRESS DEER

BEAR OF THE YEAR
and elk, rabbits, lions, birds etc.

NEW WAY TO CALL
and many other features plus fishing

"A patriarch of the cliffs and canyons, he's a trophy unique in the world, and one that should be hunted more than he is."

From "The Rocky Mountain Goat," by Jack O'Connor

As one of our oldest enemies, [the wolf has] been shot, trapped, and poisoned. But he is also one of man's most ancient friends."

The author explains that while no animal has a reputation as bad as the wolf, people must remember that – "The dog is nothing but a tamed wolf altered and twisted into odd sizes and curious shapes by selective breeding."

From "The Wolf," by Jack O'Connor

Alberta Elk —

The author and his son, Charlie, take Barbara and John LoMonaco big-game hunting about 125 miles north of Waterton Lakes National Park in Alberta. John, shown in the photograph above, takes a record-book bull that has a dark cape spotted with platinum-colored hair.

From "The Elk Wore Platinum," by Andy Russell

1962

Outdoor Life

35¢ · DECEMBER, 1962

HOW WILD ARE BOARS?
Hawaiian Hara-kiri

TRIP OF THE MONTH
Off-Season Jackpot

A FISHERMAN'S TOUR
Part II: England
by Joe Brooks

A RHINO THAT WOULD AMUSE T.R.
by Jonathan Roosevelt

MOST DANGEROUS BEAR?
I Say Polar!

KNOW DEER TO GET ONE
Even Whitetails Goof

ICE FISHING FOR TROUT
Midwinter Excitement

PLUS: Snowshoe Rabbits, Geese, Antelope

Outdoor Life

35¢ APRIL, 1962

Who Said Browns?
HOORAY FOR RAINBOWS!
A Challenge for the Experts

NEW FISHING LAWS

THAT'S WHERE I WANT TO BE
Our Editors Name Favorite Fishing Spots

BASS THEORIES EXPLODED, Part II
The Things That Do Catch Bass

SPECTACULAR MULTI-SEQUENCE PHOTOS
How to Cast Better With Double Haul

MAKE LIKE A RABBIT
Call Game Into Shooting Range

BEARS ARE WHERE THEY FIND YOU
Plus Jaguars, Antelope and Record Sheep

Outdoor Life

Ultralight — 4 Ounces!

FOR A FISHING BARGAIN
Read: We Hired A Bus

Deer Specials

▶ **OUR FIELD EDITORS PICK BEST AREAS TO HUNT**

▶ **WHERE TO HIT THEM**
O'Connor Calls The Shots

▶ **I WORK FOR MY BUCKS**

PLUS: Bears, Sheep and Elk

ART OF HUNTING MULE DEER
By BYRON W. DALRYMPLE

"Southwest hunter stalking with morning sun at his back is set for easy shot at buck mule deer that's partly blinded by sun."

In this article, the author compares hunting mule deer and whitetail deer. He writes, "The muley is a deer, like the whitetail, but that's where the similarity stops."

From "Art of Hunting Mule Deer," by Byron W. Dalrymple

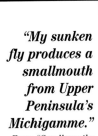

"Suddenly, one of the charging pigs caught poor Phil and tossed him end over end."

The author and Raymond Arraujo hunt Hawaii Island for wild boar that can weigh over 300 pounds.

From "Hawaiian Hara-kiri," by Lyman Nichols Jr.

"My sunken fly produces a smallmouth from Upper Peninsula's Michigamme."

From "Smallmouths Are Different," by Byron W. Dalrymple

Head-bumping Practice —

The photo above shows two young rams that "minutes earlier had run like rabbits when a mature ram caught them flirting with ewes . . ."

From "How to Stalk a Ram," by Jack O'Connor

30 Pounds and Up

MY No. 1 FISHING SPOT

By HANK ANDREWS

"If I appear a bit shaken as I hold 30-pound laker, it's because I am. I boated second 30-pounder within hour and released it."

The author writes about fishing lake trout in Gods Lake, Manitoba.

From "MY No. 1 Fishing Spot," by Hank Andrews

Outdoor Life

35¢ · JULY, 1963

NO. 1 FISHING SPOT
30-Pound Lakers

MY 40th BUCK

TROUT AFTER DARK

NEW VACATION IDEA
Fishing on The Fly

Sam Welch Report:
HOW TO CATCH
LUNKER BASS

MY GREATEST HUNTING
ADVENTURE
Cougar Nightmare

THE HUNTING HORSE
Pronounced 'Haunting'

PERFECT TROUT STREAM

Outdoor Life

35¢ · MAY, 1963

RECORD BLACK BEAR
East's Biggest
Killed in New York

THOSE BIZARRE BASS

INEXPENSIVE
VACATIONS
■ FAMILY AND FISHING?
Roll 'Em Together
■ WILDERNESS ADVENTURE?
Trailblaze A Vacation
■ TRIP OF THE MONTH
New Road to Top Fishing

Also: BEAR, TURKEY, COUGARS, RACCOONS, CARIBOU

Outdoor Life

RIGS FOR FISHERMEN
LATEST BOATING TRENDS
MOTOR SPECIFICATIONS

■ O'Connor Gets A Lion
Tragic Bear Mystery
■ Ice-Fishing for Smelt
Rams Were My Bugaboo
■ Midwinter Bird Hunt
Found: Bass Bonanza
■ Hunting by Air Photos

1963

Expert Archer —

The author hunts with expert archer Bob Lee for wild turkeys. In the left photo, Bob's arrow is about to intercept the bird. At right, Bob pulls a second arrow, fires at the falling turkey, but misses. The first shot proves lethal, however, and Bob has his trophy bird.

From "Turkey on the Wing," by Byron W. Dalrymple

"We pressed ourselves against the cliff like flies..."

The author and his fishing companion John McClary are rescued by the Air Force after they become trapped above a waterfall in the San Joaquin River in California.

From "Trapped in Devil's Hole," by Keith E. Oveson

"Scattering bamboo in all directions, the enraged beast crashed into sight five yards away from us."

From "Double Take on Elephant," by J.M. Barker

35¢ · OCTOBER, 1964

Outdoor Life

LEFT FOR DEAD
Mauled by A Grizzly

NEW GAME AREAS

FOR BEST FISHING
Plan A Hunting Trip

20 BEST DEER SPOTS IN U.S.

MY GREATEST TROPHY
by Fred Bear

UNIQUE NEW FISHING LAKE
ALSO: Grouse, Deer, Elk, Moose

35¢ · NOVEMBER, 1964

utdoor e

HOW I SHOT THE NO. 1 DEER

BEST QUAIL HUNTING

ELK ON THE ROOF

ES

UCKS

PARDY
t There!

MIRACLE OF WHITES CREEK
New Way to Repair Trout Streams

MY FAVORITE CAMPGROUNDS
by Our Camping Editor

Outdoor Life

STORIES

NEW WAY TO SHOOT WOODCHUCKS

IDEA FOR OPENING DAY
Look Southward, Angler

AMAZING PHOTO STORIES
■ Headlong Bears
■ Savage Encounter

LOST FOR EIGHT DAYS

PLUS: Spring Turkey, Ducks

"Not in 100 years, I was told, had a striped cat been killed by a bowhunter."

The author describes shooting a 350-pound tiger with bow and arrow. His first shot missed, but the second shot, which was taken at 80 yards, killed the tiger.

From "My Greatest Trophy: Tiger with an Arrow," by Fred Bear as told to Ben East

"Many hunters who have been mauled by lions are alive, but when old M'Bogo pounds a victim, he makes the job last."

From "The Cape Buffalo," by Jack O'Connor

Alligator Snapper —

The author remembers a quiet catfishing trip with his grandson Paul. Using a trotline, they mistakenly hook a giant alligator snapping turtle. They finally land the monster, which tips the scales at 114 pounds.

From "We Fought a Fresh-water Monster," by Edward Nowak Jr.

"Chatfield [the author] happily holds 41-pound chinook he's sure has won him a crab dinner."

From "Whoop-and-Holler Salmon," by Chester Chatfield

BONUS | **1965 Boats and Motors**

A CHRISTMAS GIFT OF WATERFOWL

ELK IN VIRGINIA?

35¢ · JANUARY, 1965

Outdoor Life

Cover Story: Great Little Cat

CHARGED BY A POLAR BEAR
Also: Bears With A Handgun

MOST DANGEROUS GAME
No. 6: The Rhino

LAKE TROUT AT 30 BELOW ZERO
Also: Steelhead, Barracuda

"The buffalo's sinister stare made me wish I had a machine gun instead of a bow and arrow."

The author takes a 51-day safari to Africa and shoots the following animals: elephant, leopard, three Cape buffaloes, sable, eland, zebra, two wart-hogs, red bush pig, reedbuck, and two giant lizards. He used bamboo longbows with draw weights ranging from 75 to 110 pounds.

From "The Big Ones of Africa Hit Back," by Bob Swinehart

Outdoor Life

$25 Got My Goat

MAGIC FISHING MONTH

BACKPACK ADVENTURE
We Gamble on Poison

NEW HUNTING LAWS

30 Special Photos!
HOW TO SKIN A TROPHY
Step-By-Step In Color

HELL ON AN ISLAND
A Castaway's Ordeal

BLOOD IN HIS EYE
Murderous Moose Attack

35¢ · MARCH, 1965

Outdoor Life

NEW FISHING WATERS
Fabulous Arctic Trip

JAGUAR FACE-TO-FACE
Tight Turn With Tigre

MUSKIE EXPLOSION
Ohio's Big-Fish Boom

BEAR NIGHTMARE
4 Nights of Terror

NEW WAY TO FLY CAST
Learn in 20 Minutes

MY TOUGHEST TROPHY
3 Cougars at Once

"After 800 pictures, some within three feet, I'm sure a bear will challenge me one day."

From "My Four Years with Grizzly Bears," by Norman D. Weis

Polar Bear —

The author poses with a 1,200-pound polar bear. After he shot an arrow deep into its shoulder, the bear charged and had to be shot with a gun.

From "Too Much Bear," by Art LaHa

"A big buck, neck swollen with the rut, cleared the creek in a soaring leap. I raised my .270."

From "10 Straight Years: The Way to Get Deer," by Ken Gilsvik

"The wounded bull started for us, and Barney Jawbone made tracks fast enough to make Jim Thorpe jealous."

The author, a big-league baseball player from 1914 to 1932, writes about hunting moose after the 1925 baseball season.

From "A Ballplayer's Moose Hunt," by Ray (Rube) Bressler

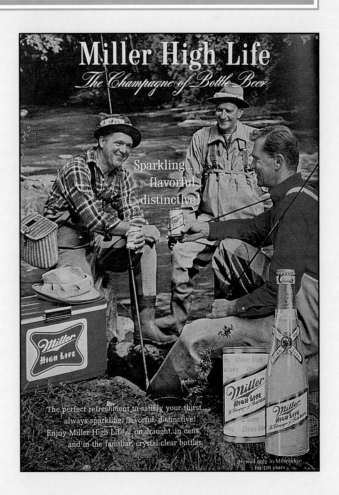

February, 1966

Outdoor Life

35¢ · FEBRUARY, 1966

A DAY ON SNAKE MOUNTAIN

THE DEVIL JAGUAR

MOST NEGLECTED BIRD

MEANEST GAME?

HOT WINTER FISHING
1: North and 2: South

DEER FOR THE RECORD
Hot Line on Rabbits

ADVENTURE IN LATIN AMERICA

Charlie Dye

March, 1966

Outdoor Life

35¢ · MARCH, 1966

HUNTING AND FISHING
New Deal for Sportsmen

BED FISHING FOR BASS

Adventure In Latin America: Part 2

NEW HUNTING COUNTRY
The Last Frontier

SMARTEST TROUT OF ALL
How I Catch 300 A Season

A DEER FOR THE RECORDS

September, 1966

Outdoor Life

35¢ · SEPTEMBER, 1966

FOUR FISHING STORIES

BOWHUNTERS' MECCA
Too Many Bucks

NEW HUNTING LAWS

WEST COAST SPECIAL
Bandtail Flyby

Scoop for Texan: Hunts Mongolia's Argali

HOW TO DRIVE DEER
Plans To Fool Bucks

THE THREAT TO HUNTING
Let's Not Kill Ourselves

WOW! WHAT A WAPITI!
Big Elk, Big Surprise

FOUND: NEW DUCK BONANZA
No. Dakota Birds Abound

"I found a new frontier for hunters when I became the first American to take Mongolia's regal rams."

The author is shown with his finest Mongolian ram. The horns measured 48⅛ and 47⅝ inches long; 20⅛ and 20 inches in circumference.

From "I Hunt Mongolia's Argali," by George H. Landreth

"Warren waits cautiously as more ducks approach Salt Lake Pass, another hotspot we hunted in North Dakota."

The author discovers lots of ducks in North Dakota on his way home from a waterfowl hunt in Saskatchewan. A year later, he returns with long-time hunting partner Warren Holmes to shoot redheads near Jamestown, N.D.

From "Found: New Duck Bonanza," by John O. Cartier

"Perched atop wave-battered rocks on the California coast, six of us took 150 stripers in a few hours."
From "Rough Water Bass," by James D. Lamon

"Fish close inshore, use superfine rigs, jig easy, and come running when someone yells the magic word."

The photo to the left shows ice fishermen in action on Sandusky Bay, Ohio.

From "New Things in Ice Fishing," by Ken Mason

Kansas' First Deer Hunt —

Above, the author shows his nontypical whitetail, which is a candidate for the Pope and Young record book. Below, Buck Minium, left, with his whitetail and Larry Bell, right, with his mule deer. The author tells of the 1965 Kansas deer season, its first in modern times. The announcement meant that all 50 states would now offer deer hunting.

From "Kansas' First Deer Hunt," by Al Weaver

BONUS | 1967 Boats and Motors

FISHERMAN ABROAD

AMAZING BEAR PHOTOS

JANUARY, 1967 35¢

Outdoor Life

THINGS TO READ AND DO NOW:

- Hare Hunting ▪ Ice Fishing
- Crow Shooting ▪ Quail Ditto

THE JAGUAR FOLLOWED US:

Record Deer: Fun Duck Hunt

Summer-Run Steelhead —

The author writes about the fantastic summer fishing for steelhead in six rivers in southwestern Washington. The fish range in size from 4 to 14 pounds, and angling pressure is almost nonexistant. In the photo to the left, Ken Kennedy of Longview, Washington, brings in an exhausted "springer" – an early summer-run steelhead.

From "Boom in Steelheads," by Rex Gerlach

Outdoor Life

Mule Deer, Whitetail
Where You Hunt Both

Fall Steelheads Back
Plus Southern Fishing

The Football Knee
Unusual Elk Story

Bears Look For Trouble
Also: Grouse Shooting

Alaska's Tough New Game Code
Hits guides, planes, hunters

Duel In The Rockies
Bighorn fight photos

Best Duck Bargain In U.S.?
It's for free!

Outdoor Life

AUGUST, 1967 35¢

Found: A Bass Bonanza
FANTASTICO'S THE WORD

Pike and Grayling

Hunting's Big Mystery
WHAT HAPPENS TO PHEASANTS?

New World Record
Tarpon On A Fly

Another World Record
RAGE OF A BEAR

How To Fish The
High Lakes Now

Who Says Hunting's Finished Around Here?

Al Pfluefer and John Emery team up to boat shark. They use a small outboard skiff for general inside fly fishing."

The author explains how a new breed of fly fishermen are taking large shark and amberjack off the coast of Key Largo, Florida.

From "Revolution in Salt Water Fishing," by George X. Sand

"I show tarpon after our 1¾-hour battle in the Belize River."

The author takes a trip with long-time fishing partner Bill Cullerton to the western Caribbean on the coast of British Honduras. Fishing both the Belize River and the British Honduras flats, they catch tarpon, bonefish and snook with flies and plugs.

From "Troublesome Tarpon," by Tom McNally

"Glade Ross, on left, congratulates me on mule deer. Big buck was partially hidden in heavy brush, but he showed up in 6X scope."

The author floats the Green River in Utah's Desolation Canyon with guides Ron Smith and Glade Ross. They hunt chukars, ducks and deer, and fish for catfish and trout.

From "Meet Me on the Green," by John S. Flannery

Phil's Trophies —

The author takes his 17-year-old son Phil on an Ontario big-game hunt a few days before Christmas, 1966. Phil is shown above with his special bonus trophy, a black timber wolf. In the photo to the left, Phil walks up on the bull moose he dropped minutes after his dad took a cow moose for the freezer.

From "Special-Extra Moose Hunt," by Lt. Col. H.J. Samuels

1968

The Al Goerg Story: A Hunting Tragedy

MAY 1968   35¢

New Fishing Laws
Walleyes In Maytime

Outdoor Life

How To Catch More Trout
By Joe Brooks

Vacation Adventure: Part 2
Alaska's Inside Passage

I Shot A Record Deer
Also: Cougar, Lynx

Bass Worth Waiting For   Spring Turkey Hunt

"I lift the great ram's ponderous head where he fell after 800-yard shot."

The author obtains a permit from the Royal Government of Afghanistan to take one Marco Polo ram.

From "Greatest Trophy of All,"
by George H. Landreth

FEBRUARY 1968   35¢

Close Call
for Moose

Outdoor Life

The Trouble with Grizzlies
Also: End of A Deer Jinx

The Postwar Cartridges
by Jack O'Connor

2 Ice-Fishing Stories
Plus: Fishing The Keys

What Do You Know About Guns? | Varmint Shoot

Big Monthly Report On YOUR Region

OCTOBER 1968   50¢

Outdoor Life

here To Find The Hunting
Pages On YOUR Area

ow To Outsmart Deer
so: Pheasant, Quail

eatest Trophy Of All
re Marco Polo Sheep

Wildlife Bombshell
ho Owns The Game?

is Subject of Guns...
ow Our Family Uses Them

NEW: Joe Brooks Now Outdoor Life Fishing Editor

Frogging —

The author tells of frogging after dark with Yves Moreau (above), nicknamed "Frog-dog," in the bayou country of southern Louisiana.

From "Bullfrogs in the Bayous,"
by Wandell Allegood

"I land this 13-pound char on my McNally Magnum."

The author says if you're looking for trophy-size fish in either fresh- or saltwater, you should try huge streamers that imitate real baitfish.

From "The Giant Killers,"
by Tom McNally

20-Pound Steelhead —

The author is shown above with the biggest steelhead he has ever caught on a fly. He writes, "That small bullet-shaped head was made for boring into heavy currents." "An overall sheen of silver spoke of months at sea . . ."

From "Heaven Is a Steelhead," by Joe Brooks

"As his partners ran from their caribou kills, the big black wolf lunged at the intruding grizzly, biting him hard on the back."

From "Wolves Don't Live by Rules," by Frank Glaser as told to Jim Rearden

WOLVES DON'T LIVE BY RULES

1969

FEBRUARY 1969 50¢

Outdoor Life

Bears I Have Known
Rabbit, Bobcat Hunts
Also: Winter Quail

Crappies All Year

Are Our Duck Laws Outdated?
Flyway Concept Exploded

Was Elk Hunting Ever Like This?

New Ice-Fishing Method
For Big Northerns

A Hunter Trapped · Bargain Safari for Photographers

Under VC Guns · August Deer Hunt

JULY 1969 50¢

Outdoor Life

Nightmare Spring
100 Bass a Day?
Trout: East & West

's Paradise
's Budget

Midnight

Best Fishing in Canada · That Bear Again!

wo Deer Stori

Outdoor Life

Hounds and Rabbits

Getting Along With Grizzlies

Too Big to Hang
Elk Hunter's Elk

Run for the Blue Water
New Kind of Fishing

Spectacular Bass Photos Explode Old Theories

"Judie takes a solid grip on .22 handgun . . ."
The author takes his wife Judie on a bobcat hunt with guide Eldon
Berman and his Bluetick hound, Huck.
From "Judie's Cat," by John R. Higley

164

"I heft part of a last-day catch ready for filleting."

The author tells how his fishing group takes a 10-day trip to Mirond Lake, Saskatchewan, for $94.70 per person.

From "Fisherman's Paradise on Workingman's Budget," by Gerald W. Bowers

"The King, filmed on Serengeti Plains, looks contented with his domain. You'll need long telephoto to get shot like this."

From "Picture It: A Bargain Safari," by Erwin A. Bauer

"We find sporty upland game birds and a deer apiece among the river breaks across the wide Missouri."

From "An Unforgettable Hunt," by John O. Cartier

"This home-modified version of big-reservoir fishing boat has bow fisherman in best possible position to make accurate casts."

From "Bright New Look in Bass Boats," by John Oney

By Jack O'Connor: Elephants on the Zambezi

JANUARY 1970 50¢

Outdoor Life

1970 Motors & Boats

Best Antelope in 70 Years

2 Ice-Fishing Stories

Deer, Crows, Doves, Moose

More Olive Fredrickson Adventures: Bears!

Best Of The 1970s

EVENTS, BOTH IN AND OUT OF CONSERVATION CIRCLES, FELL OVER ONE ANOTHER IN THESE YEARS THAT WERE FLYING TOWARD THE END OF THE TWENTIETH CENTURY.

Indications were that the unpopular war in Vietnam would soon end and we could look once more toward some peaceful years. The United States celebrated its 200th year as a nation. Investigators disclosed that President Richard Nixon was involved in a burglary of the Democratic National Committee headquarters at Watergate and Nixon became the first president to resign his post in what the Democrats termed a "national disgrace." The Three Mile Island nuclear power plant malfunctioned and released radioactive gases into the atmosphere, but with slight damage and concern outside the news media reports.

Of special interest to hunters, bird students and conservationists was a ban on the use of DDT in the early 1970s. This chemical had long been spread as a poison to kill insects that fed on man's cultivated crops. Researchers then discovered that both song and game birds that fed on insects killed by DDT were also victims of this chemical and the ranks of our feathered population were growing exceedingly thin. The increase in bird numbers was obvious after DDT was declared illegal.

For more than twenty years I had been ranging two continents in search of stories for *Outdoor Life*, which now, after three-quarters of a century, continued to be recognized as America's premier hunting and fishing magazine. During that score of years Bill Rae continued as *Outdoor Life's* third editor. His background and

expertise helped to keep the magazine on a high quality level.

When I reached the age of 65 in November 1972, I was due to retire from active duty and be staked out in the back pasture. Bill Rae postponed my retirement date for another year to keep me on his staff as long as he was editor. So it wasn't until the next year that my name was scratched off the regular payroll.

For the remainder of this decade and well into the 1980s, I worked on a free-lance basis, but was kept as active as I had been as a full-time employee. I continued to gather regional news for that feature and to make trips for material, pictures and stories, all of which were handled on a free-lance basis.

Five years after I retired as a regular staff member of *Outdoor Life*, I made my final big-game hunt into the high country of the West. This safari proved to be my most difficult of a lifetime spent chasing after big-game animals. And one of the reasons for this was my age. I was just stepping over my 73rd milestone.

But age was not the only factor that made this my most difficult trip. For almost six weeks we combated the lofty, roadless wilderness in northern British Columbia. We often were gone sixteen or more hours from camp. After a dawn breakfast, we'd trail a dozen or more miles to a mountain or valley our guide considered best for moose, sheep or mountain goats. We'd stay in the saddle until the slope became so steep that the horses could not climb any higher. We'd picket them there and proceed afoot up terrain so precipitous that it was necessary to climb with our hands and arms as well as with our feet. I'm sure we went up and across mountain slopes that any intelligent wild sheep would have avoided. There were times at those altitudes when my lungs and body were so starved for oxygen that I didn't think I could pick up my foot for another step.

During the six weeks in this near-vertical wilderness, our outfitter estimated that we were in the saddle for a total of some 600 miles. I am positive that we climbed another 600 miles afoot.

Through the years, my hunting and fishing activities for *Outdoor Life* kept my body hard and physically fit. I was in good condition for this hunt and while there I ate like a starved lumberjack, but my carcass lost almost twenty pounds.

After Bill Rae's retirement, *Outdoor Life* went through a succession of editors in an effort to seat one capable of filling Rae's ample shoes. Most of those trial editors had the ability and talent, but for personal and other reasons, each new editor stepped aside after only a short time in office. Through this period, the editorial staff, field personnel and department editors continued to publish an excellent magazine that gave the readers stories and departments that were entertaining and informative.

By the end of this period a few long-time contributors, such as Byron Dalrymple, David Richey and George Laycock, continued to furnish stories, and some of the durable department editors, like Ben East, Erwin Bauer, Jerry Gibbs, and David Duffey, were still aboard. Some of the others, like the seemingly perennial Jack O'Connor, who had given up his seat on the firing line to Jim Carmichel, were no longer on board.

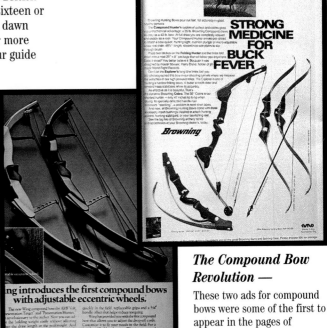

The Compound Bow Revolution —

These two ads for compound bows were some of the first to appear in the pages of *Outdoor Life*. The Browning ad appeared in 1974; the AMF Voit ad, 1977.

February 1970 50¢

Outdoor Life

High Climb for Bears
A "Spoiled" Cougar

The Cliff-Hanging Lion
"Night Out" for Ice Fishermen
Track of the Whitetail
Arctic Adventure: A Seal Hunt
Now's a Time for Bass
Mountain Grouse Are Work
Hunting in Iran
Fly for All Season

"Eleanor [Jack O'Connor's wife] and I stand near ponderous bull that I dropped with a brain shot from .416 Rigby as it lumbered toward me at 15 yards."

From "Elephants on The Zambezi," by Jack O'Connor

Hiked In 68

Outdoor Life

Is It Taps for Wild Alaska?
Smallmouths Hit Now
June Hunt: I Came for Bear

Spectacular Photos: Games Whitetails Play

Are Hunters Murderers? Look at the Record

AUGUST 1970 50¢

Bass and Catfish
Wild Goose Hunt
Longfin Tuna Run

Outdoor Life

Bears Don't Always Run
How to Catch Big Muskies
A Bowhunter's Goat
New: No-Hackle Dry Fly!

High in the Velvet: A 'Summer' Deer Hunt

"I ran for the open fields as fast as my legs could carry me, but when I looked over my shoulder, that sow was gaining fast."

The author tells of her childhood on the Athabasca River in Alberta, Canada. She writes, "Some of my bear encounters were funny. Most sent chills down my back."

From "Bears in My Hair," by Olive A. Fredrickson

"Throwing sticks into trees, we tried to persuade the soggy birds [doves] to fly."

From "Watch Who You Call Birdbrain," by Nord Riley

"I crouch behind my urial, an Asiatic wild sheep, that I dropped at 200 yards in northern Iran. Horns taped 37¹/2 and 36 inches."

From "Hunting in Iran," by Erwin A. Bauer

"At my shot the bull laid back that huge rack and barreled over the bog."

The author remembers a trip he took to eastern Ontario for moose. While he and three other hunters wait for bush planes to pick them up after completing a 6-day hunt without seeing a moose, the group spots two moose in the distance.

From "Last Call for Moose," by Chester Anderegg

1971

Jack O'Connor: How to Choose an Outfitter

AUGUST 1971 60¢

Outdoor Life

The Strange White Deer
Backpack & Float Trips for Trout
The Elk Paid Me Off
Winter with North Country Red
Bass & Muskie Fishing

Nightmare: A Hunter's Fight Against Death

The Nonresident License Gouge

DECEMBER 1971 60¢

Outdoor Life

How to Look for Whitetails
Free-for-All Ducks
Record Caribou for Bow

Fight! Elk and Deer Tangle
Moose Ten Feet Tall
N.Y. Ice-Fishing Bonanza

Jungle Adventure in Ceylon · Bobwhite Leftovers

"The safari hand was killed. Croq was wounded, and Constantino was knocked senseless."

A "dream safari" suddenly became a horrible nightmare beset by six brutal murders.

From "The Day the Rebels Attacked," by Eduardo Martinez Ochoa as told to Oscar Brooks

The Day the Rebels Attacked

Camping—

Outdoor Life

Bowhunt for Chucks
Spring Chinook Fun

New Ice-Fishing Action
Never Say Never About Bears
Best Bass Bait in World?

Safaris in the Seventies Will Be Different

170

"*Rick stalked in a long half-circle to the left and then slowly raised his .270 for the 150-yard shot.*"

The trick for this Colorado hunter wasn't just to find a goat, but also to make sure it was a billy.

From "Don't Shoot the Bearded Lady," by Dan Gravestock

This Happened to Me!

Hunter's Downfall
A TRUE TALE by Delbert Dawson
Murray, Utah

WE PAY CASH FOR ALL TRUE ADVENTURES PUBLISHED

I was packing out a two-point buck that I'd shot near Mt. Nebo in Utah, when I came to a 20-foot falls. Trying to pick my way down the cliff, I made a misstep

As I fell I shoved the deer aside and grabbed for brush, but I got only air

I hit under the falls with a jolt and felt the deer crash down on top of me

Dazed, I crawled out. The iciness of the water made me feel numb all over

I managed to drag the buck out of the churning pool. Then I was running . . .

. . . for my truck. Brush clawed at me, and I fought a powerful urge to sleep

It was dark when I reached the truck. I drank whiskey and coffee, then . . .

. . . changed to dry clothing. I was so numb I had to slice my boot laces off

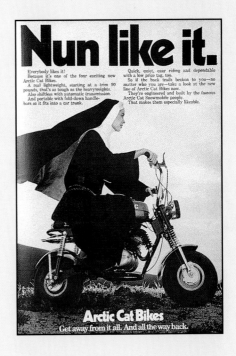

AGE BONUS: BEST FISHING IN YOUR AREA

APRIL 1972 60¢

Outdoor Life

THE COLUMBIA: A RIVER
ON ITS DEATHBED

THE NEW FISHING LAWS

A RECORD BEAR FOR
MICHIGAN

DRIFT FOR SMALLMOUTHS

GODS COUNTRY:
LAKERS, NORTHERNS
AND WALLEYES

THE GREAT CROWBAR CAPER

HUNTER OHOS IN NEW ENGLAND   SPRING TURKEY HUNT

NEWS OF YOUR REGION

Great Shots I've Missed — by Charles Elliott

JANUARY 1972 60¢

Fastest Duck Shooting

1972 BOATS & MOTORS

Winter Steelhead Tips

Outdoor Life

Mauled by a Buffalo

The Mystery of Diablo Hill

Doubling Up on Elk

Ice-Fishermen's Snowfari

A Lesson in Sheep Hunting — by Jack O'Connor

Outdoor Life

WE CALL UP BEARS
AND LIONS

BIG BASS AT MIDNIGHT

O'CONNOR MAKES LAST
SHEEP HUNT

MISSINAIBI NIGHTMARE

VACATION
PARADISE FOR
TROUT

DEER HUNTING IN AUGUST

WHEN IN TROUBLE USE NYMPHS   CAMPOUT CAMPUS

"One shot ended my lifelong search for a major big-game trophy I did not have."

From "The First for O'Conner: Salmon River Whitetail," by Jack O'Connor

"The great bull was suddenly right out in the open, and we drew and released almost in the same instant."

Scoreless after years of bowhunting, two hunters pull off a unique double play on a royal bull elk.

From "One for the Book: Trophy for Two," by Harry E. Troxell III

"As I leaned forward I caught my toe on a root and fell headlong in front of the coiled rattlesnake."

From "Don't Break Your Tushes on Me, Snake," by Jimmy Fuller as told to Ben East

"The narrow-gauge locomotive brakes to a halt to pick us up for the return trip."

From "Railroad Time Is Fishing Time," by Karl R. Zimmermann

"The sow reared erect and swung her paw as I stumbled backward into the lake."

Angels would fear to tread where this trapper had to go to get at a furious sow bear that he still sees in his dreams.

From "Fools Plunge In," by Earl J. Fleming

Outdoor Life — August 1973, 60¢

SPORTSMEN'S FEAR: MUST THIS LAND DIE?

NEWS | 8 PAGES ON YOUR REGION

COVER: PERILS OF A HUNTING GUIDE

HERE COMES BASS BLITZ

THE BIG PIKE YOU CAN DRIVE TO

SHOW YOUR KIDS OUR GREAT OUTDOORS

REACHING HIGH FOR TROUT TREASURE

SALMON'S BRIGHT LIGHT · FIRST DOG UP

"If you can strum this last tango for worms, you'll never dig them again."

Sam Potter strokes while H.C. Juedes hunts. Their team tied for first place in the Worm-Fiddling Championship with 37 worms.

From "Worm-Fiddling Championship," by Frederick G. Behrnes

Outdoor Life

O'CONNOR: WHY

CONFLICT: MAN AND SALMON

RAM UNDER THE RIM: BIGGEST BIGHORN

A TETON ADVENTURE: TROUT IN SPRING

MAGNOLIA TURKEY HUNT

CON THE WARY BASS

THE NEW FISHING LAWS

BIG WALLEYES · FLIES FOR LUNKERS

Outdoor Life — January 1973, 60¢

JACK O'CONNOR HITS AT GRAND SLAMS

NEWS | 8 PAGES ON YOUR REGION

THE SPRING WE MOVED THE MOOSE

INCREDIBLE DEER HUNT

SQUEAKING UP THE RED FOX

NEW BOATS AND MOTORS

QUAIL & GOOSE HUNTS; FISH FRY ON ICE

Look at OUTDOOR LIFE 75 Years Ago

175

NEW FISHING TACKLE: JERRY GIBBS REPORTS

Outdoor Life

NOVEMBER 1974 60¢

NEWS
8 PAGES on Your Region
HOTSPOTS · PHOTOS · MAPS

Cover Story:
HOTTEST DEER AREAS IN U.S., CANADA

BASS & TROUT HIT SUPER LURE

ANTIHUNTERS ARE SNEAKING IN THE BACK DOOR

GOOD CHANCE TO DIE: CARMICHEL

CALL DUCKS AND SCORE

NOSTALGIA: "AIN'T NO SUCH ANIMAL!"

MAY 1974 60¢

Outdoor Life

NEWS
8 PAGES on Your Region
HOTSPOTS · PHOTOS · MAPS

COVER STORY
FLOAT TRIP TO

CARMICHEL BUCKS

BASS: REPORT ON NEWEST WAY TO FIND 'EM

Outdoor Life

DECEMBER 1974 60¢

Cover Story:
CAMP NOW AND HUNT SNOWSHOE RABBITS

ORDEAL HUNT: CLIFFHANGER IN FREEZING HELL

DEER HUNTING EAST AND WEST

HOW TO BACKPACK FOR HOT ICE-FISHING

HOW "MR. PIKE" CATCHES LUNKERS IN NEW HOTSPOT

EXCLUSIVE YELLOW SECTION
8 PAGES NEWS YOUR REGION

"Bill Hoxie, whose idea of a great retirement is to fish every day all year, watches as George Dorrell hauls fish."

This article tells how expert fisherman Bill Hoxie spurns the crowd's copycat techniques and mythic hot holes.
From "He Tracks Down Winter Bluegills," by John O. Cartier

"Three of the 23 successful hunters show results of Vermont's turkey program."
From "These Yankees Hunt Wild Turkeys Again," by Ted Janes

"The range was 10 yards, but I still hoped for a miracle to save us and the elephant."
The author writes about the 11th day on his first African safari when he faced a crazed elephant.
From "Good Chance to Die," by Jim Carmichel

" 'Lord what a mink!' Dad exclaimed. He lifted the animal up and examined it, his face still registering disbelief. 'Biggest ever I knowed of,' he said."
From "Ain't No Such Animal," by Farrel Dablemont as told to Larry Dablemont

"After my fish is released, I watch Ron's sailfish leaping at the boat after nearly 40 minutes of fighting."
Four anglers share their tale of fishing the Gulf of Papagayo, off Costa Rica.
From "A Coast of Riches: Billfish Alley," by Ted Kerasote

"Herb Benjamin works goose call from behind silhouette stand."
From "Don't Make Waves! Up to Our Necks for Geese," by Michele Caraher

"Coyote is puzzled; the hunters are stymied. Coyote came between caller (background) and gunner. It escaped because safe shot was impossible."

From "How to Get Amazing Results from Your Coyote Call," by Byron W. Dalrymple

WHITETAILS, MULEYS: TROPHY-TAKING TIPS

Outdoor Life
NOVEMBER 1975
75¢

Cover Story
HOW YOU CAN
FIND MORE
DUCK HUNTING

FLYRODDING Without Flies

Hunt for Big SQUIRRELS

Warning: RATTLERS Ahead!

Foul-Weather GUN Care

"U.R." —Rabbit Hunter
Extraordinary

GUNS FOR '75 • GUIDE TO SPINCAST REELS

Outdoor Life
MARCH 1975   75¢

COVER STORY
BEST FISHING
IN AMERICA?

BASS: Where, How
on 3 Top Lakes

How to Fool a
GOBBLER Now

Dream Trip for
Monster PIKE

2 Great Treks
to High-Country
TROUT

Tough Hunt
for Desert RAM

EXCLUSIVE YELLOW SECTION
8 PAGES OF NEWS
YOUR AREA

EXCLUSIVE YELLOW SECTION
NEWS OF YOUR AREA

Outdoor Life
JANUARY 1975   60¢

Cover Story:
THE GRIZZLY
SHOWDOWN

BASS AGAINST
ODDS: HOW TO
FIND PATTERN

DEER:
BLACKPOWDER
IN BONUS SEASON

DANGER: RAM HUNT
ON THE ROCK WALL

SALMON SNAGGING:
THE BATTLE RAGES

EXCLUSIVE YELLOW SECTION
8 PAGES ON
YOUR AREA

"Control line wrapped around his hand, Frank leaped from the runaway sled and was yanked 10 feet through the air."
From "Frank Glaser: Adventure Was His Life," by Jim Rearden

"We risked our lives to get a shot at an Iranian ibex. But then I blew the shot – or so it seemed."
From "At Russia's Doorstep: Horns That Make Your Heart Skip," by Jim Carmichel

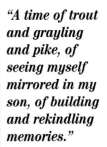

"A time of trout and grayling and pike, of seeing myself mirrored in my son, of building and rekindling memories."

The author tells how he brought his 11-year-old son, Steve, to Manitoba on his first fishing trip away from home.
From "The Fever Is Contagious: Hooked for Life," by Nick Karas

"The wolves closed in fast, and then one attacked from each side, two from behind."

The author remembers how 50 years in the Saskatchewan bush taught him how to survive and how to see and understand wild things.
From "A Hunter Remembers," by Ted Updike

DECEMBER 1976 75¢

Outdoor Life

Where to hunt, fish in your region

25 facts to improve your **RABBIT** hunting

The <u>ideal</u> **BASS** boat

Award-winning fight to expose PCBs

How champion flyrodders get those record sportfish

Small creek **TROUT**

Winter Action!
One man's Arctic survival
"Selective" ice-fishing
Stunning wildlife photos

How I bag more **DUCKS** now
Plus: Will success spoil goose hunting?

E: NEW WAY TO TRACK BASS

WHERE T HUNT & FISH IN YOUR REGION

utdoor Life

JUNE 1976 75¢

ry: The **CATFISH:**
r a reputation

nt System rking?

How anti-hunters try to kill Jersey whitetails

yer secret of a fabulous **TROUT** fly

BONUS REPORTS
Canoe camping Raccoon
hunt Mushroom facts
Pros, cons of baitcasting
eels Buying a
used camper vehicle

---

6 BOATS & M

Outdoor Life

JANUARY 1976 75¢

COVER STORY
hotographing **BEAR**
t close range

ow to hunt
OX in winter

better ways to
ANFISH from shore

linch when you
hoot? How to stop

super vacation
dea for **BASS** now

Build your own pond
Venison recipes

experts tell their flycasting secrets

"Photographers are trying for a shot of a bear off to their left. They never realized there was a kibitzer."

In the author's opinion, a portrait photograph of an Alaskan brown bear is a fine trophy. But you can put your life on the line trying to take it.

From "Too Close for Comfort," by Buckley Winkley

Guns are Unloaded —

"... a handful of plantations still provide the gentleman's game for those who value quail the way they used to be. Among them is Longleaf Plantation near Lumberton, Mississippi ..."

From "Gentleman's Game," by Bruce Brady

"To a wildfowler, the arrival of autumn's first flock of honkers is a signal event."

In this article, the author discusses the dramatic increase in Canada goose populations since the end of World War II, but also the serious problems caused by their overcrowding on refuges.

From "Will Success Spoil Goose Hunting?" by J. Phillips Knight

"Once – then again – the fish came out of the water. The second time it seemed to hang there for a moment, its gills flared in defiance."

From "The Belligerent One," by Jerry Gibbs

Typical Plant and Animal Life Found in a Limestone Stream —

From "A Tale of Two Waters," by Vince Marinaro

"A northern pike about to take a yellow perch while a duckling flees for its life."

From "King of the Weedbeds," by Jerry Gibbs

AUGUST 1977

STILL ONLY 75¢

Outdoor life®

Where to hunt, fish in your region

STEEL SHOT MAKES NOW!

FISHING'S hot

Arctic by canoe

hunter's guide estands

s of the Amazing s show BASS

COVER
The colorful **COUGAR** -- endangered by man, or new danger to man?

Argentina Brookies —
"Against an awesome backdrop of soaring peaks and sprawling glaciers, [Ernie Schwiebert], the man I considered to be the best flyfisherman in the world, put on an exhibition of power and grace equal of Ted Williams, Rod Laver, and Sam Snead in their salad days."

From "The Boca Brookies," by Peter Miller

Outdoor life

Where to hunt, fish in your region

How birds show you where fish are

Why is famed fisherman Lefty Kreh giving up on his short rod?

men outdoors: Why they nt a better deal...now

ts for **ANTELOPE, TURKEY, RABBIT**

t-yourself lderness trips

's new ng gear

DECEMBER 1977 $1.00

Outdoor life

Where to hunt, fish in your region

We must harvest does or lose our **DEER** herds

COVER STORY
Make a tent camp your hunting base

DUCK hunt ordeal: 16 hours of terror

SHOTGUN PERFORMANCE: Facts that count on loads, choke, patterns

My backyard **BASS** lab - new facts on bigmouths

Antelope Camp —

The author tells of a successful antelope hunt on public land in west-central Wyoming. Both he and his wife shot respectable bucks.

From "Double on Antelope," by Erwin A. Bauer

MY OWN BERMUDA TRIANGLE

I battled the tough yellowfin for three hours, and dreams of a line-class record danced through my head. Then a spoiler showed up—16 feet long. By BOB STEARNS

"I battled the tough yellow-fin tuna for three hours, and dreams of a line-class record danced through my head. Then a spoiler showed up – 16 feet long."

From "My Own Bermuda Triangle," by Bob Stearns

un-endangered species

Pronghorn Antelope: 1925—Estimated 13,000 to 26,000 in U.S.A. Today: Minimum population in all western states is 500,000.

Presented by the National Shooting Sports Foundation and approved by the International Association of Fish and Wildlife Agencies.

"Finally I met my guide. He's a friendly chap, dressed in a green jumpsuit plastered with patches. Apparently he is a 'field tester' for everyone . . ."

From "Bass Guides I've Known and Hated," by John Weiss

Pronghorn Antelope —

This one-page editorial explains how game numbers in America are abundant due to the efforts of state wildlife agencies and the financial contributions by hunters through license fees and special taxes. For example, in 1925 there were 13,000 to 26,000 pronghorn in the U.S., but today [1977], the minimum estimate is 500,000.

From "Un-endangered species," by the National Shooting Sports Foundation

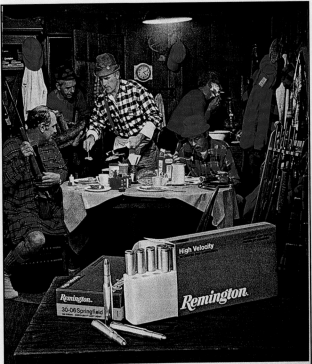

1978

NEW YORK, PENNSYLVANIA, QUEBEC, MAINE
Guide to ice fishing
DECEMBER 1978 $1.00

Outdoor Life

LICENSE $ $ —
DO WE GET
OUR MONEY'S
WORTH?

HUNTING
Deer ■ Quail ■ Squirrels
Foul-weather shooting

FISHING
Hot new rig ■ Update: Bass, Trout

FIRST RESULTS...
A radical plan to nab poachers

COVER STORY
The Great Horned Owl:
Nature's Flying Tiger

in COLORADO   Ducks in LAKE TEXOMA
Pheasants: DAKOTAS, KANSAS, NEBRASKA
NOVEMBER 1978 $1.00

Outdoor Life

GRIZZLY'S
LY CHARGE
for DUCKS
RABBITS

DEER
SPECIALS
Hunting
crowded areas

Guide to
asing scents

Outdoor Life

Where to
fish, hunt
in your
region

FLY IN TO WILDERNESS ACTION
Fish, hunt, camp on your
own—Where and how

Spotting DEER: How to
sharpen your woods vision

The charging moose left
me for bear bait

Catch the water wolves—
Pike, Pickerel, Muskie

PHEASANT · GEESE
BASS · TROUT

*"You are paying a lot of
money for wildlife, but is it
blown away by politicians
with no professional
training?"*

*From "The Struggle for
Your License
Dollar," by Dr.
George Hulsey and
Bill Vogt*

"... and he bears down on his victim like a freight train. Often the victim is large, for the mako burns fuel like a blast furnace."
From "MAKO!" by Pat Smith

The 5 Stages of the Midge's Life Cycle —
"The midge pupae were rising to the surface from the huge moss and silt beds of the cutoff's slower, more protected area. Feeding on them were hundreds of rainbow trout . . ."
From "Small Flies for Big Trout," by Dave Whitlock

"I pounded the hooks home again. That did it. The muskie responded by throwing itself high into the air in a twisting, barrel-rolling leap."
From "The Fever Spreads South," by David Richey

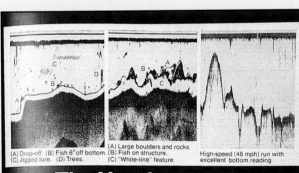

4-lb. 10-oz. Bluegill —

Coke McKenzie is shown holding his former world-record bluegill. He caught the fish in 1947 from Ketona Lake in Alabama. Coke was using 6-pound-test nylon line and a limber cane pole. In the background photo, the author is shown using the sneak method that helped Coke catch his record bluegill.

From "The Sneaky Truth about Big Bream," by John E. Phillips

"Up from the ocean depths, into the great rivers [the salmon and steelhead] come. Danger and death lurk in every mile they swim."

From "Valor of the Run," by Jerry Gibbs

". . . all the bear had to do was bite down on my leg and jump out of the tree . . . and I'd fall to the ground where she could rip me to shreds."

From "Sow Bear Attack," by Jim Heiney

"In a world of self-proclaimed [fishing] experts, Gadabout Gaddis was a breath of fresh air."

From "Gadabout Revisited," by Pat Smith

GADABOUT REVISITED

For 20 years his television show fascinated 20 million people. Where is Gadabout today?
By PAT SMITH

"These iron-tough trout [steelhead] that boil in from the wide-open seas have provided the finest angling moments I've ever known."

From "Hats Off to the King," by Clare Conley

JULY 1980 $1.25

OUTDOOR LIFE®

MIDWEST MAGIC!
Dark-Night Browns

In Search Of GIANT CROCODILES

SPECIAL SECTION
Air Powered Arms

Profile Of An Obsessed Angler

JACK O'CONNOR
Tribute To Our Greatest Hunter

Best Of The 1980s

DURING THIS DECADE, THE EARLIER EFFORTS TO IMPROVE HUNTING AND FISHING IN AMERICA SEEMED TO COME TO FULL FRUITION.

The wild turkey population, which had been almost exterminated in many regions, was now so abundant throughout the nation that most states had generous turkey seasons. The whitetail deer herd that had been shot down drastically during the early part of the century had become so numerous by the 1980s that, in many sections, they foraged on fruit and farm crops, ate local gardens down to the roots and were considered a nuisance.

Regulations continued to exist, but in most states they were extremely liberal, with seasons extending from bow hunting days in early fall and continuing through the winter. Limits were most liberal. In one state, Alabama, hunters could shoot one deer each day of the ninety-day season.

Some species of big-game animals that were at low ebb in certain sections were restocked and protected by refuges and closed seasons. The hunting of animals considered to be in no danger of extermination was allowed, but with the exploding number of hunters, a reduced number of hunting days and other restrictions were in order. Prized big-game trophies like mountain sheep, grizzlies and elk were, in many states, available only to hunters who made application months ahead of season and were fortunate enough to draw a permit.

In the 1980s, the do-gooders, whose cult keeps itself alive by creating dissatisfaction with the way we live, launched a campaign against hunting and hunters. The rallying point was that killing animals for sport was a form of murder almost as sinful as taking a human life.

In the last decades of the century this issue blossomed into a hate campaign. The self-styled humanitarians held meetings —usually over ample steak dinners– to decry how wicked it was to end any God-given life and to declare war on all hunters.

These sentiments boiled to a climax in the 1980s. On many occasions the anti-hunters barged into areas where legal hunting was allowed and made movements or created loud noise to frighten the game animals away from where a hunter stalked or waited.

In some regions this became such a common occurrence that states found it necessary to pass laws, with fines and sentences, to curb this annoyance. When the courts stepped in, most of the illegal harassment came to an end.

For some obscure reason, the campaign against taking the lives of wild creatures did not include fish. In the early portions of this century, game fish of all kinds were so plentiful, they were considered inexhaustible. No attention was paid to size or limits. As I heard an old negro fishing friend say, "If he's big enough to bite my hook, he's big enough to eat."

After the middle of the century, anglers began to be aware that fish caught on each trip were fewer in number and were not as large in size as those taken a few years before. When this finally dawned on the fishing clan, its disciples took the initiative and began to do something about it. They opened a campaign, both verbally and though the pages of *Outdoor Life* and similar publications and in the newspaper outdoor columns, to carefully handle hooked fish and return them unharmed to the water. This became a policy of the fishing contests and tournaments, with winning points given for all fish released alive and unharmed. This practice spread and, by the end of the 1980 decade, seemed to be generally accepted by the angling fraternity.

Legislation and regulations continued to be enacted in most of the states. While Alaska was still a territory, it had passed its first game measure with specific protection for Kodiak bears. The national refuge system, which had started with Florida's creation of the Pelican Island bird reservation in Indian River, continued to

spread throughout the nation. As our population increased, a greater number of men and women moved outdoors to enjoy their recreation.

Even with the dramatic increase in licenses—especially out-of-state—the number of people investing in them had swelled through every decade except those during the war years when our sportsmen were off in other parts of the world seeking a different quarry.

A large part of the increase in our game resources can be credited to those people who hunted and fished and who enthusiastically supported the excise taxes on outdoor equipment paid by manufacturers and dealers, though they knew that those taxes would be passed on to them through the profit-and-loss system. They accepted the price increases because the law specified that the money from these excise taxes would be used to employ technical staffs in the wildlife departments, to create federal refuges, federal hatcheries and game farms and to set aside vast areas to produce an abundance of game on huntable lands.

Another large role in these developments was played by *Outdoor Life* and other hunting and fishing periodicals. They carried their hunting and fishing stories as usual, but also devoted much space to the promotion of those state and federal functions that needed the verbal support of their readers.

Hunter Harassment —

This article details several events of hunter harassment by anti-hunters. In the illustration above, a group of hunters in the Spatsizi wilderness in British Columbia face anti-hunters who have locked arms to block the trail.

From "Anti-Hunters vs. Hunters: War in the Woods,"
by Richard Starnes

1980

OUTDOOR LIFE
PACIFIC EDITION

HOLIDAY SPECIAL
Christmas Goose

**VOLCANO'S Impact
On Fish and Game**

**SURF: Frontier
For Steelhead**

**BONUS: Hunting
For Giant Bucks**

OUTDOOR LIFE
MIDWEST EDITION

Getting Wise
To Ringnecks

Black Bear with
A Predator Call

CARMICHEL: Our
Greatest Guns

**BONUS REPORT
Our Spookiest Bucks**

OUTDOOR LIFE

NEW YORK: Fishing
The City's Reservoir System

Shad Roundup for the
NORTHEAST

FUELING: The Serious
Side of Firearms

SPECIAL SECTION:
Pages of Fly-fishing

Hope for the
ATLANTIC SALMON

BASS LURES:
The 5 Reliables

*"Is the next world-record largemouth bass really
worth its weight in gold?"*
From "The $1,000,000 Bass," by John Phillips

White Shark —

"If you hook him, the great white knows exactly what to do. He makes no move in panic. He will test you and your tackle to the breaking point, then keep what he thinks he needs in reserve to kill you."

From "Giants of the Deep," by Jerry Gibbs

"Chukar partridge, a bird of the dry, wild highlands."

From "Upland Birding in the Golden West," by Larry Toschik

"No bowhunter had ever killed a desert ram in modern times, and I was setting out to be the first."

From "Once in a Lifetime Ram," by Brad Siefarth as told to Dwight R. Schuh

"In a few isolated instances, however, the results of the unregulated netting were plain."

From "Showdown on Indian Netting," by Ben East

"Seasons were not for gunners like me, men who hunted for birds they could put on a Christmas Day table to feed their families."

From "The Christmas Goose," by John N. Cole

John N. Cole Wins 1979 Conservation Award —

Cole's book *Striper – A Story of Fish and Man* arouses public indignation about the near extinction of the great game fish. President Jimmy Carter presents the award. Looking on are Mrs. Cole and *Outdoor Life's* editor, John Culler.

1981

"No wonder the Crees and Ojibwas call the northern pike the snake, the water wolf and other similar names."

From "In Search of the Water Wolf," by John Weiss

JUNE 1981

How To Decoy Buck Deer Right To You!

OUTDOOR LIFE

STILL ONLY $1.25

MIDWEST SPECIAL FEATURES

How And Where To Fish The New Lake-Trout Hotspot

Tricks That Take Big Muskies Quickly

How To Get More Crappie Now

How To Fish A Lake You Don't Know

Where You Find Big Fish In The Weeds

JANUARY 1981 $1.25

OUTDOOR LIFE

MIDWEST EDITION

CARMICHEL: Hunt For A Giant Kodiak

World's Best Fishing Reels

Shocking Facts About Poaching

Icefishing Devils Lake

Ohio Grouse At New High

OUTDOOR LIFE

STILL ONLY $1.25

EAST Special Features

PENN.—Got A Deer Yet? Here's How To Have One Last Chance

8-STATE ROUNDUP—Where To Bow Hunt Late Season Deer

N.Y., N.J., CONN.—Big Cod Are In. Here's How To & Where To

ME., N.H., VT.—Where Hare Are

N.Y., N.J.—Brant How To

Wild Bow Hunt For A 500-Pound Black Bear

40 Fun Questions To Test Your Bass Fishing Know-How

New Humor Column By Pat McManus See Last Page

Trophy Elk —

"Clarence Brown shows the magnificent rack of the bull elk that he shot in 1977. It is the best elk trophy since 1899 and scored 419⅝ Boone and Crockett points. The bull was taken near the Panther River in Alberta."
From "Best Elk in 82 Years," by Clarence Brown as told to John O. Cartier

"Any mammal larger than a mouse was BIG game."
From "My Africa," by Paul Quinnett

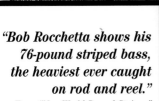

"Bob Rocchetta shows his 76-pound striped bass, the heaviest ever caught on rod and reel."
From "New World-Record Striper," by Bob Rocchetta as told to Al Ristori

"An incredible two million deer and countless other game are killed every year by poachers."
From "Socking It to the Poachers," by George Laycock

1982

URKEY DECOYS—Should You Use Them or Not?

OUTDOOR LIFE

FEBRUARY 1982

$1.50

McMANUS HUMOR:
See Last Page

SOUTH
pecial Features

EXAS—The State's
2 Top Bass Lakes

RKANSAS Walleye

LORIDA—Great Rabbit
unting Open To Public

ow To Catch Lots Of
ats In The SOUTH

he Worm That Drives
LORIDA Tarpon Crazy

BASS STORIES
ow To Use Spinnerbaits
ou Can Log Your Way To Lunkers
ow To Make Your Own Bass Lures

YOUR FOREST FOR SALE? See List

OUTDOOR LIFE

DECEMBER 1982 $1.50

ow to Hunt
ARM BUCKS

u Can Hunt
K ON YOUR OWN

ESE—Smarter, But
u Can Fool 'Em

ve THE LAST LAUGH
th Pat McManus

IDWEST Features

e-Season DUCKS

CHIGAN Thumb Hunt

NSAS Rabbits

WA Pheasants

ISCONSIN Crappies

BEST PLACES TO GET YOUR DEER

OUTDOOR LIFE

SEPTEMBER 1982 $1.50

m Carmichel's
ecrets For
HITETAILS

ow To Tell A Trophy Buck

IDWEST Deer Hunting
Reports:

ICHIGAN, ILLINOIS,
INNESOTA, OHIO,
ISCONSIN, IOWA,
ISSOURI, INDIANA,
NSAS, NEBRASKA,
RTH & SOUTH DAKOTA

*"I ended my
verbal barrage
with a challenge:
'You might as well
come out and
watch me bleed
to death, you
yellow S.O.B.!' "*
From "I've Been
Shot!" by Mac Elder

"Coming full tilt right at me was the grizzly. I have no recollection of that next instant, although I did become airborne and fly across the fire . . . "

From "Moment of Terror," by Michael A. Ganger

"He was not only the weirdest buck I'd ever seen, but, as I'd soon learn, the smartest."

From "Old Crooked Horn," by Lew Littleton as told to Jim Zumbo

"The good news is that complete protection has brought the alligator back . . . the bad news is that gators are killing dogs and people."

From "Jaws That Are Real!" by Frank Sargeant

The 1981 BASS Masters Classic —

This Al Hirschfeld illustration shows, clockwise from right, second-place winner Harold Allen, Pat McManus, Roland Martin, Bobby Murray, Ray Scott and first-place winner Stanley Mitchell.

From "The BASS Classic Caper," by Patrick F. McManus

How To Hunt Real TROPHY TURKEYS

Outdoor Life

MARCH 1983 $1.50

America's Best TROUT FISHING
- Deadly Grizzly Attack
- How To Catch Night Bass
- Real Rabbit Dogs Are Back
- Dangerous Varmint Calling
- New Riflescope Roundup

WEST Features
- CALIFORNIA Trout
- WASHINGTON Albacore
- OREGON Big Trout
- COLORADO Walleyes
- UTAH Black Bear
- MEXICO For Bass
- WYOMING Golden Trout
- IDAHO Smallmouths

"He [Wayne Davis of Sheridan, Arkansas] got a 10-point buck last season when he rode his bull into thick undergrowth, flushed the big whitetail, dismounted and shot it."

From "This Hunting Story Is No Bull," by W. Horace Carter

W TO USE S

Outdoor Life

FEBRUARY 1983 $1.50

Where And How To HUNT COUGAR
- ...ring Gobblers Are Dumb
- ...ecrets Of The Walleye Whiz
- ...ew Way To Fool Bass
- ...est Way To Catch Spring Trout

WEST Features
- ...LIFORNIA Brant
- ...EELHEAD Highway
- ...LORADO Trout
- ...KE MEAD Stripers
- ...ONTANA Trout
- ...LUMBIA R. Sturgeon
- ...LIFORNIA Trout
- ...AH Smallmouths

How An Average Hunter Always Gets Elk

Outdoor Life

DECEMBER 1983 $1.75

- Carmichel Tells Why You Miss Ducks
- How To Shoot **RUNNING DEER**
- Snowtime Is The Best Time For Deer

EAST Features
- PENNSYLVANIA Late Deer
- LONG ISLAND Waterfowl
- NEW HAMPSHIRE White Perch
- NORTHERN TIER Snowshoes
- NEW JERSEY Quail
- DELAWARE Cod/Tautog
- MARYLAND Ducks

McManus Gets The Christmas Spirit

> *"Fifty-five cowboys on horseback and 70 Navajo braves on foot set out to drive 10,000 deer . . . It was stupendous but, when it was over standers posted to count the deer had a tally of exactly none."*
>
> From "The Biggest Deer Drive Ever,"
> by George Laycock

40-pound-plus King Salmon —

"Jim Teeny catches and releases several hundred steelhead each year. And he does it by using some unorthodox tricks that go against the well-established rules followed by loyal steelhead anglers."

From "This Man Throws Rocks at Fish,"
by Jim Zumbo

> *"When a foot appears in its face, that big old catfish will often grab it. When it does, nearly everyone in the creek will know because the fish puts its body into it and the whole creek vibrates."*
>
> From "Grabbin' Cats," by Frank B. Selman

Peak For A Trophy Ram

A near-fatal crash shattered my leg, but not my determination to hobble into the mountainous backcountry for a trophy Stone ram. Little did I realize that my torturous hunt would end at the bottom of a gorge with one for the books.

By Bill Heuer as told to John O. Cartier,
Editor-at-Large

In 1978, I was driving my old Army-type jeep down a Pennsylvania mountain when the brakes failed. I knew the road well enough to know I couldn't make the turn at the bottom of the slope.

I figured that I'd be a dead man for sure if I didn't jump, so I bailed out. I landed in a ditch with an awful crash, rolled and tumbled, and finally came to a stop on my stomach just in time to see my jeep going end over end down the mountain. When my head began to stop spinning I sat up and saw

ILLUSTRATION BY KEN LAAGER
continued on page 86

> *"A near fatal crash shattered my leg, but not my determination to hobble into the mountainous backcountry for a trophy Stone ram."*
>
> From "Peak for a Trophy Ram," by Bill Heuer as told to John O. Cartier

WEST

CALIFORNIA Trout • WASHINGTON Mule Deer
OREGON Chukar • IDAHO Deer • SAN FRANCISCO Ducks
MONTANA Antelope • COLORADO Quail

OCTOBER 1984 $1.75

Outdoor Life

You Can
**HUNT
PHEASANTS**
Better Alone

How To Hunt Deer
In Bad Weather

Special Report
On New Hunting
Apparel

Make Scrapes
That Fool Bucks

A Dog For Turkeys?

Cheaters For
More Trout

726598

*"If you're just an opening-weekend
pheasant hunter, you're missing out on
some of the best shooting of the year.
Late-season rooster rousters will find
lots of elbowroom and, better yet, plenty
of pheasants."*

From "Snowtime Roosters," by Tom Huggler

MIDWEST

WINTER Walleyes • MICHIGAN Whitetails
MISSOURI Ducks • NORTH DAKOTA Coyotes
OHIO Bluegills • IOWA Deer • WISCONSIN Rabbits

DECEMBER 1984 $1.75

Outdoor
Life

We Miss
Game

Bauer:
He Got His
**GREATEST
PICTURES**

ter Hunting
e Snow

unt Snowshoes
ithout A Dog

ych Up A Buck

McManus Reveals
he Christmas Mystery

726598

Outdoor
Life

Bonus—8 Pages On
New Camping Trends

Best Bait For
BIG BASS?

Know Your Weather
To Catch More Fish

Are Rainbows Smarter
Than Brown Trout?

MIDWEST Features

WISCONSIN Wilderness Fishing
OHIO Bass
MICHIGAN Salmon
MISSOURI Stripers
ILLINOIS Muskies
KANSAS Bluegills
IOWA/ILLINOIS Bass
ONTARIO Trophy Muskies

**McManus Admits
Fear Of The Dark**

726598

Fishing's Newest Magic Box

Now a space-age radio computer can steer anglers to underwater action.

Remember the old one about cutting a notch in the gunnel of your boat so you can find the spot again where you caught the big fish?

Now it's true—and you don't even need a knife or a wooden hull. All it takes is a little box the size of a big book. You just push a couple of punch keys on the front of it and you're in business. The gadget instantly memorizes where you are and, anytime you want to return to that exact spot on the lake, for example, to try to catch another lunker, it steers you right back to the same place—as if it had memorized the street address of the chunk of water where that fish lived.

continued on page 146

By Bill McKeown, Boating Editor

LAKE MICHIGAN

"... it steers you right back to the same place–as if it had memorized the street address of the chunk of water where that fish lived."

From "Fishing's Newest Magic Box," by Bill McKeown

Greatest Catch

By Donald Millus

The tiger shark was 10 times heavier than the muscular stonemason who was bracing his 190-pound, six-foot body against the shark's first run. His 16/0 big-game reel paid line grudgingly and his heavy rod bent in a tight arc as the shark surged away from the pier with a huge hook imbedded in its jaw. A multistrand, wire leader and 130-pound test line connected the shark with the man who was out to set a world record that still stands—and do it from a fishing pier, not a well-equipped boat.

It was the afternoon of Saturday, June 13, 1964, and the

continued on page 140

"The tiger shark was 10 times heavier than the muscular stonemason who was bracing his 190-pound, six-foot body against the shark's first run."

From "Big Game Fishing's Greatest Catch," by Donald Millus

"The Armistice Day storm brought with it the kind of shooting that makes a water-fowler forget the bite of the wind. But by the time the hunters realized the storm's ferocity, many had already died – frozen to death in their blinds."

From "The Day the Duck Hunters Died," by Chris Madson

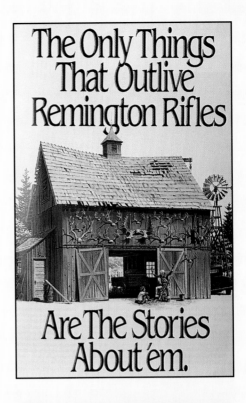

EAST

Catch Opening-Day TROUT In PENNSYLVANIA
Where To Hunt Spring GOBBLERS In NEW YORK
Plus Stories On: WEST VIRGINIA, NEW JERSEY, MARYLAND

APRIL 1985 $1.75

Outdoor Life®

Where To Catch
BIG BROWN TROUT

Anti-Hunting Is Being
Taught In Our Schools

Little Tricks That
Take Big Bass

Stormy-Day Deer
Hunting Can Pay Off

Pat McManus Finds
The Fountain Of Youth

New Hotspot For
Giant Rainbows

*"But after we loaded [the crocodile] aboard . . .
and headed for camp . . . one of the croc's eyes
opened and I realized that it was still alive. That's
when the engine quit."*

From *"The Croc That Wouldn't Croak,"* by Jim Carmichel

eer Hunti

NOVEMBER 1985 $1.75 $1.75

Outdoor Life®

...ightening Story
...A Real
...EAR ATTACK

...w To Hunt Farms
...r Big Deer

...ew Fishing Lure
...olor Selector:
...es It Work?

...ur Pat McManus
...ead "The Last Laugh"

...ow To Be Super Successful
...Your Big Game Hunting

MIDWEST

Best Places For WISCONSIN Deer
MICHIGAN Trophy Bucks
OHIO Whitetails

New Bear Repellents That Work!   Still Only $1.75

DECEMBER 1985 $1.75 $1.75

Outdoor Life

...oon Charts For Fishing:
...nake Oil Or Not?

**How You Can
Stalk CLOSE
To Game**

...cience Makes Trolling
...roduce More Fish

...est-Selling Humorist
...at McManus On Last Page

...unt Swamps Now For Big Deer

WEST

Where To Hunt Wild CALIFORNIA Hogs
Best Spots For DENVER-Area Geese
Use A Muzzleloader On OREGON Whitetails

A World-Record Rack —

The author with his Colorado pronghorn that scored 85 points, tying the Pope and Young world record. He took the buck from a pit blind overlooking a water hole.

From "World-Record Pronghorn," by Judd A. Cooney

Teen Trophy —

The author started hunting when she was 8 years old. Now 16, she has taken a moose, a caribou, a grizzly and a Dall ram.

From "Teenage Trophy Hunter," by Heidi Reakoff

"I wanted to score on my first buck, but got more than I bargained for. That muley's antlers were so cumbersome that I wanted to leave them behind. Thanks to mom, I didn't, and my deer just may help rewrite the record book."

From "Bowhunting's No.1 Mule Deer?" by Bill Barcus as told to Lee Kline

1986

Outdoor Life — AUGUST 1986 $1.75

How To See More Game When You Hunt

$1.75

ow To Hunt Today's
MART MULEYS

roven Ways
Super Hunter
ETS BIG DEER

ish Up To Your Waist In
eeds And Get Big Bass

ow To Track
eer And Get Results

uaranteed Ways To Get Doves

cManus Writes Fear Of Floating

State-By-State BOWHUNTING FORECAST
Best Waters For PENNSYLVANIA Pickerel
LAKE ONTARIO Smallmouths • LONG ISLAND Marlin

AST

$1.75

Outdoor Life — JANUARY 1986 $1.75

s Ears And How To Fool Them

Still Only
$1.75

reating
AZED
AR?

ifle Right
ame? See
HEL'S RATINGS

y Best Time To
tch Bass—If It's Legal

st—Seller McManus
asts Icefishermen

ADLIEST BAIT For Trout

Best Winter Trout Fishing In PENNSYLVANIA
Top Spot For NEW YORK Snowshoes
NEW JERSEY Neglected Icefishing Hotspots

AST

Outdoor Life — MAY 1986 $1.75

pecial FIS

ow To Smoke The
sh You Catch

ow To
ake Bass
t Night

arn Fishing From
Tapes—47 Fishing
deos Reviewed

icks That Take
mallmouth & Walleye

pecial Camping Section

cManus Finds Out About Women!

The Mississippi Comes Clean
KENTUCKY's Stream Fishing For Muskies
Plus Stories On: VIRGINIA, TEXAS

OUTH

Montana Grizzly —

The author tells how two bird hunters
thought they were safe chasing pheasants 50 miles north of Missoula. That was
before they stumbled upon a "beehive of
rampaging grizzly bears."

*From "A Nest of Grizzlies," by
John Haviland*

Minnesota Heavyweight —
Noble Carlson holds a 10-pointer that field-dressed at 240 pounds. His unusual methods for tracking whitetails were summed up by the author: "Moments earlier, we had been half-trotting right on top of a deer trail. Now he [Noble] was yapping at me to be totally silent. Tracking deer, Noble Carlson-style, is weird."

From "A Noble Way to Track a Buck," by Jeff Murray

"Running a wild river is like a game of cards, with blind fate, dumb luck and the will to live deciding the outcome."
From "Stranded in a White-Water Hell," by Gary Miltenberger as told to Kitty Pearson-Vincent

"And if the game wasn't dangerous enough, Paul Rainey made it so by jumping an enraged polar bear or riding to hounds with Arican lions as the quarry."
From "A Millionaire's Dangerous Game," by Jim McCafferty

1987

"Chuck Yeager's an ace at everything from dogfights to salmon battles."

From "Fishing with the Right Stuff," by Jim Zumbo

Discovered—How To Call Deer

$1.75

FEBRUARY 1987 $1.75

Outdoor Life

How To Catch
RIVER WALLEYE

How To Hunt The
7 Toughest Turkeys

Guaranteed Dirty Tricks
That Take Trout

Proven Ways To Catch
Bass From Clear Water

CIAL DEER HUNTING YEARBOOK

New Treatment For Deadly Snakebite

$1.75

JUNE 1987 $1.75

Outdoor Life

ree State Stories Below

ow To Catch
MIDWEST PIKE
n Bass Lures

our Safety
omes First
urkey Hunting

ow To Read
ature's Signs
o Better Fishing

cManus' Law:
t Can't Be Done."

azy Deer Hunting
icks That Get Results

MIDWEST WISCONSIN/MICHIGAN Bears
MINNESOTA Walleyes • INDIANA Bass
ILLINOIS Largemouths • OHIO Pike

SEPTEMBER 1987 $1.75

$1.50

DISPLAY UNTIL
NOVEMBER 1, 1987

Outdoor Life

r Hunting Report
e Details On:

AN, OHIO, ILLINOIS,
OTA, WISCONSIN,
MISSOURI, IOWA,
& SOUTH DAKOTA,
NEBRASKA

Three New
unting Stories

Can Afford

Hunt Farm Squirrels

e How-To
eally Works

Grizzly Attack —

On June 24, 1987, Louis Kis from the Montana Department of Fish, Wildlife and Parks was releasing a 500-pound adult grizzly from an aluminum live-trap. As the photo sequence shows, the bear reared up for Louis after the trap door was opened and pulled him to the ground. Louis, with no other options, quickly pulled his revolver and shot the bear.

From "The Grizzly Attacked!" by Richard P. Smith

"Bob Foulkrod packs out a Pope and Young record caribou."

The author tells of a lengthy hunt he took with Bob Foulkrod to Quebec and Labrador. Bob took four record-book caribou with bow and arrow.

From "Four-Of-A-Kind Caribou," by H. Lea Lawrence

Dream Hunt —

The author writes, ". . . I'll bet that more hunters dream about and drool over bull elk than buck deer." He then explains what is needed to have a good elk hunt without spending a ton of money.

From "Elk on Your Own," by Ron Spomer

1988

Cover 1 (top left):

AKEBITE SHOCK CURE—PART 2

$2.00

JULY 1988 $2.00

Outdoor Life

The Story Of Famous American BEAR HUNTERS

HOW TO CATCH LOTS OF MIDWEST BASS

MIDWEST Local Stories
MICHIGAN'S Lake St. Clair
WISCONSIN Pothole Bass
OHIO Catfish
GREAT LAKES Salmon Tactics
ILLINOIS Catfish
MISSOURI Squirrels

Know Your Trees; and More Deer

McManus' Guide to Garage Sales

NEW INFO

Cover 2 (top right):

How To Hit Western Deer On The Run

$1.50

Outdoor Life

The Man Who Caught 140 Bears Bare-Handed

WEST Local Stories
Canada Geese
OREGON Hungarians
Pig Hunting
COLORADO Pheasants
Cutthroats
MONTANA Grouse
Corner Bucks That Beat Muleys

How To Find Grouse In All Seasons

Discover The Truth About Women And Men Hunting Together

McManus Explains Removing Hooks From People

Cover 3 (bottom left):

Outdoor Life

How To Catch Southern CRAPPIES & WARMOUTHS

SOUTH Local Stories
FLORIDA Bass
CAROLINA Trout
GEORGIA Bass
TENN. Hotspot
OKLA. Bass

FAMOUS BEAR HUNTERS
Facts About Amazing Bear Men Of The Past, Six-Part Series

HOW I GOT STARTED HUNTING
by President Jimmy Carter

Just For Laughs, Read PAT McMANUS On Last Page

Caption (bottom right):

"Ben Lilly often chased a bear with a dog tied to a rope around his waist."

The author writes of Ben Lilly, "Some called him a superhuman hunter. Others said he was a goofy old coot. Whatever the opinion of the man, there's no denying his passion for killing bears."

From "The Great Bear Men: Part I," by Paul Schullery

"*That deposited lead shot poisons waterfowl is a proven fact. And the shrinking waterfowl populations won't support lead shot for very long.*"

From "An Appeal for Steel," by Lonnie Williamson

"*Come spring, the most effective approach to walleyes is often made from shore. And fishermen who know proper technique are often waist-deep in fish.*"

From "Walleyes in Wading," by Jeff Murray

Fishing the Delaware —

"Mostly, the river skunks you. Gradually though, you notice that you're starting to catch more and better fish. Intimidation becomes intrigue. Then, you discover that you're in love or something like it, foolishly and hopelessly, with one of those manifestations of the infinite that don't even know you're there."

From "Big Water, Little Men," by Frank Conaway

HOW TO GET NEAR TO DEER

DECEMBER 1989 $1.95

Outdoor Life

Special
SOUTHERN Issue

EXCLUSIVE
REPORT

Great Lakes
Salmon ARE
NOT DANGEROUS
to Your Health

Finding Overlooked Elk

DAVE WAD

HOW TO FIND AND CATCH THE BIGGEST BASS

MARCH 1989 $1.75

CANADA
$2.25

Outdoor Life

MIDWEST REGION

EARLY SEASON
MIDWEST TROUT

Jack O'Connor's Letters, Part II

The New Rage in Turkey Calls

SPECIAL

Outdoor Life

ROMANCING
LOVE-TIRED
LARGEMOUTHS

How to Find Trout
In Any Stream

WESTERN Issue

"*Sprawling across the U.S./Canada border, this 1,980-square-mile chunk of real estate is the embodiment of what we call pristine northwoods wilderness.*"
From "Lake Of The Woods," by E.L. "Buck" Rogers

Bachelor Group of Musk Oxen —

"From musk ox to mule deer, from Alabama to Alaska, you can legally hunt year-round when you use a camera body and lens to stalk your game."

From "Lights, Big Game, Action," by Erwin A. Bauer

A Woodsman Remembers —

The author writes how Murphy, who has the antlers from 36 bucks to his credit, remembers his "best buck" as the trophy he let walk by because it was headed toward a young hunter.

From "Murphy's Pride," by Perry Johnson

"Pat McManus is *Outdoor Life's* **resident rib-tickler, and countless readers willingly offer their ribs to be tickled."**

"As with any popular entertainer, however, people often want to know more about the one who brings them so much fun. If you keep on reading, you may learn more about McManus than you ever wanted to know."

From "Inside Pat McManus," by Mitch Finley

hunting, his sobbing wife would have had no reason, on this autumn day, to be red-eyed and dressed in mourning. Folks in her neighborhood understood that in a frontier community people had to stick together. They spoke quietly of her loss and offered words of condolence. They promised help with her
continued on page 80

It was all a man could ask of his funeral—a man who so loved the sport of hunting deer that he was even willing to die for it.

The Mourning After

"It was all a man could ask of his funeral – a man who so loved the sport of hunting deer that he was even willing to die for it."

From "The Mourning After," by George Laycock

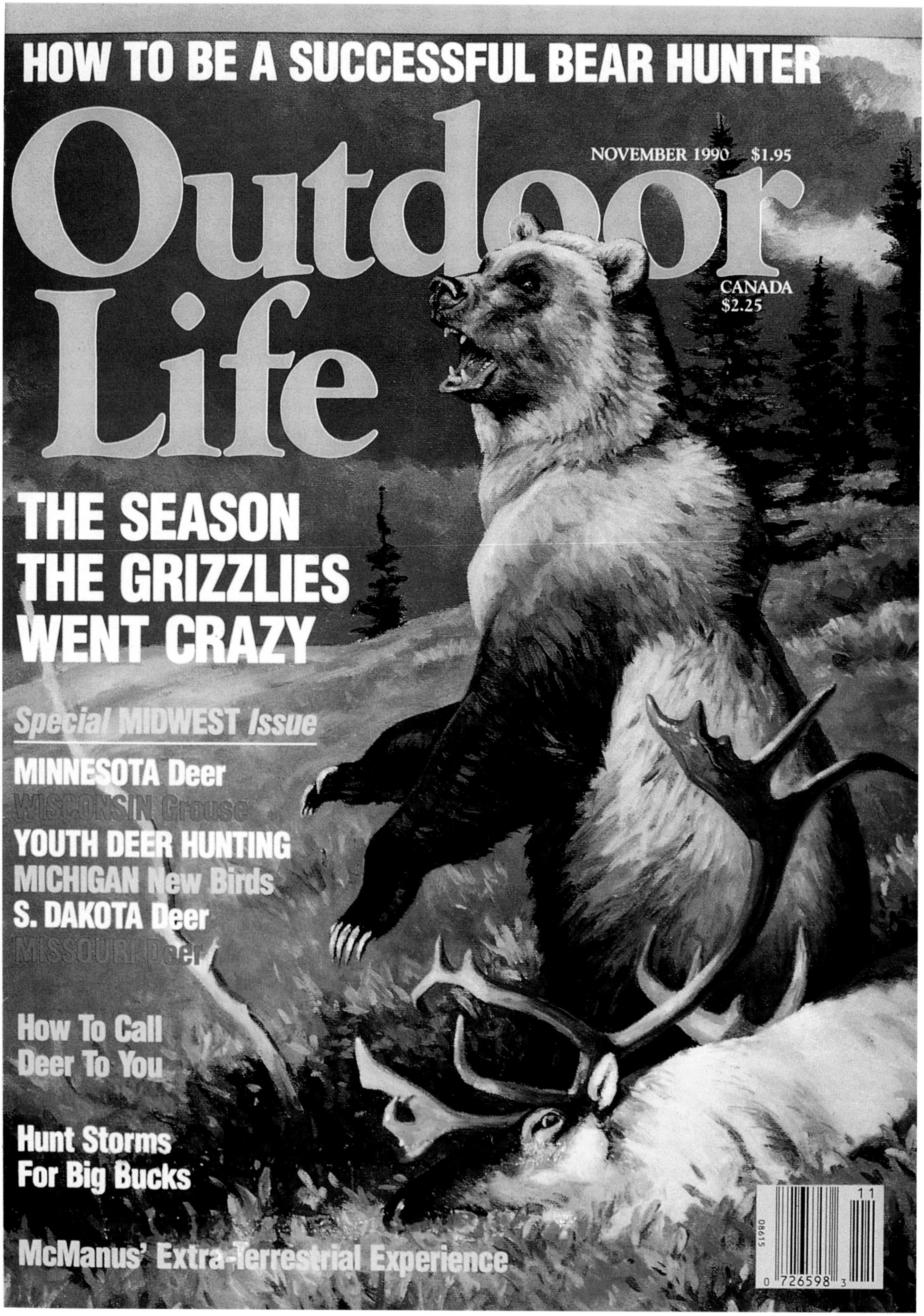
HOW TO BE A SUCCESSFUL BEAR HUNTER
Outdoor Life
NOVEMBER 1990 $1.95
CANADA $2.25
THE SEASON THE GRIZZLIES WENT CRAZY
Special MIDWEST Issue
MINNESOTA Deer
WISCONSIN Grouse
YOUTH DEER HUNTING
MICHIGAN New Birds
S. DAKOTA Deer
MISSOURI Deer
How To Call Deer To You
Hunt Storms For Big Bucks
McManus' Extra-Terrestrial Experience

Best Of The 1990s

MANY CHANGES HAVE OCCURRED IN THIS LAST HALF CENTURY SINCE I SAID "I WILL" WHEN EDITOR RAY BROWN ASKED ME IF I WOULD BE HIS SOUTHERN FIELD EDITOR.

At that time *Outdoor Life* was the property of Popular Science Publishing Company. Later it was sold to Times Mirror Company and was the first of the strictly outdoor magazines to be purchased by one of America's premier newspaper corporations.

Over the years the office staff, field personnel and regular contributors retired or passed on to happier editorial worlds. The new offices changed several times to more ample locations and working conditions.

Even with these and other changes, *Outdoor Life* retained the high flavor of its hunting, fishing, adventure and other outdoor stories and its hard-hitting editorials, all of which kept it on the throne as America's leading outdoor magazine.

People make a magazine. I was not the only member of the field staff with years of strenuous activity encountered on our assignments for *Outdoor Life*. We often stayed in the saddle from before daylight until long after dark. We climbed twelve-thousand-foot-high mountains to stalk game. We half-congealed through weather far below freezing (on one of my ten-day hunts in northern Canada, the thermometer never climbed higher than forty-five degrees below zero). We slept in the open on frozen ground and survived raging river torrents and lived to tell our more prudent readers about it. Many covers were based on such experiences and were a promise to the inside pages.

The excellence of the stories and reports in the nation's most popular outdoor pages continued into the last decade of this century and through the last years of *Outdoor Life's* trail to its one-hundredth anniversary.

Early in the 1990s, Vin Sparano, who had become a member of *Outdoor Life's* office force in 1961 as an associate editor and who, after Bill Rae's retirement, had carried a heavy share of the editorial load during those years when management was experimenting with editors, took over the job of editor-in-chief.

In 1997, Sparano retired and Todd W. Smith, who had guided one of the nation's other outdoor magazines into the top brackets, was selected to step into Sparano's big shoes. Smith, with his able right hand, Bob Brown, swung into the saddle to rein *Outdoor Life* through the last years of the century.

Very young though I was when I first lost my heart to *Outdoor Life*, I was especially intrigued by the magazine's cover each month. Much later in life I realized that the attractive covers were chiefly for the purpose of selling the book to subscribers and on the newsstands, and there is little doubt that they contributed to the phenomenal success of America's best and most popular outdoor magazine.

Of my many contributions to *Outdoor Life* over more than half a century, some of those which gave me the largest slice of pride and satisfaction were several of my colored photos selected by the editor as covers.

One of my favorites, the January 1959 cover (right), was taken in the Yukon Territory where we hunted for six weeks in the roadless and unpeopled wilderness close to the Arctic Circle.

My guide, leading a packhorse with a rack of huge antlers lashed on its back, was passing across a gravel bar just as a brilliant rainbow appeared in the sky. With my camera in hand, I jumped off my horse and ran to a spot on the gravel bar where I could make a picture of the end of the rainbow touching down in the trophy rack.

Today, that photograph means vastly more than just a scene snapped in Canada's far northern Yukon Territory. It seems more like a reflection of the beauty and drama of those years when I followed the distant game trails where no modern man had ever left a track.

That picture could be the epitaph of a life spent beyond the ends of the trails where I often stood in awe at the beauty and music of the universe, and felt at times as though I were holding hands with Eternity.

Best of all, it seems to sum up my life as a player on the super team of *Outdoor Life*, where I felt always that I had reached the pot of gold at the end of the rainbow.

WOMEN GO OUTDOORS IN A BIG WAY!

DECEMBER 1990 $1.95 CANADA $2.25

Outdoor Life

SIX DEER DRIVES THAT DON'T

Special MIDWEST Issue

ROUNDUP OF LAST
CHANCES TO HUNT
WISCONSIN Coyotes
OHIO Steelhead
MISSOURI Geese
NEBRASKA Trout

How To Hunt Honkers:
50 Ways That Work

McManus Was A "Teenager From Hell"

HUNT HARASSERS EXPOSED, COMPLETE REPORT

OCTOBER 1990 $1.95 CANADA $2.25

Outdoor Life

FOUR BIG DEER STORIES
Mule Deer Ways
Hunting In Rain
Thick Cover Bucks
New Way To Call Deer

A Message From
President Bush, Pg. 20

Special MIDWEST Issue
Six-State Pheasant Forecast
MICHIGAN Salmon
MINNESOTA Salmon
WISCONSIN Deer
OHIO Blackpowder Deer
MISSOURI Turkeys

See Funnyman Pat McManus, Last Page

The Legendary Taimen —

The author, left, and Buzz Ramsey, right, pose beside
their two Russian companions and Buzz's 80-plus
pound taimen. In describing the fish the author writes,
". . . at first Buzz thought he had hooked an underwater log. Then the surface exploded as the nearly six-
foot-long taimen completely cleared the water."

From "Russia: Fishing the East," by Larry Schoenborn

.700 Nitro Express —

"The effect was not like being kicked on the shoulder, but of being hit all over." "The recoil of heavy-
caliber rifles has been described by some writers as
a 'push.' With the .700 Nitro, such a silly description
doesn't apply unless having a 130-pound sandbag
dropped on you can be called a push."

*From "The Day I Shot the .700 Nitro Express,"
by Jim Carmichel*

When snows deepen, you'll have to meet hares on their terms. Snowshoes will become vital equipment."

The author tells of hunting snowshoe
hares with hounds in the dead of winter
in northern Michigan.

From "Hare Bawls," by Tom Huggler

Anti-Hunters Take Note: We Are Winning!

Outdoor Life

OCTOBER 1991 $2.00

CANADA $2.25

PHEASANT KNOW-HOW
Buck The Myths And Get More Ringnecks

Deadly Lures For Fall Fishing

DEER DECOYS Believe It Or Not—They Work!

SOUTH TEXAS Doves • KENTUCKY Deer
FLORIDA Rabbits • VIRGINIA Swans
ALABAMA Deer • OKLAHOMA Turkeys

ANIMAL RIGHTS OR HUNTING: WHAT'S BEST?

Outdoor Life

APRIL 1991 $1.95

CANADA $2.25

How To Catch MORE FISH: DON'T WADE

EAST Local Stories
PENNSYLVANIA Trout
NEW YORK Trout/Bass
NEW JERSEY Crappies
W. VIRGINIA Bass/Crappies
MARYLAND Turkeys
DELAWARE Shad
MAINE Trout

Best Gun When A Grizzly Charges

Get Ready For The Spring Bass Attack

How To Call Turkeys: A Friction Story

"Those who call themselves 'animal rightists' have forgotten that nature doesn't care about rights."

From "Animal Rights vs. Hunters," by Walter E. Howard, Ph.D.

"A fish big enough to sink a boat doesn't come along too often unless you're after flathead catfish."

From "Fat 'Heads," by Paul M. Liikala

"Here it is – Bob Crupi's 22-pound .16-ounce largemouth."

The author writes about how George Perry's legendary world-record bass from 1932 is in jeopardy of being topped by some huge largemouths being caught in California.

From "Biggest Bass in 59 Years," by Jerry Gibbs

1992

EXPOSED: NUCLEAR POISONING OF OUR RIVERS

OutdoorLife
A TIMES MIRROR MAGAZINE

APRIL 1992 $2.00 CANADA $2.25

TOUGH-WATER TROUT
CATCH FISH WHEN OTHERS GIVE UP

10 WAYS TO FOOL SPRING BASS

HOW TO WIN BOAT-SIDE BRAWLS WITH ANY FISH

SOUTH
TEXAS • BASS
GEORGIA • CRAPPIES
ARKANSAS • GOBBLERS
FLORIDA • BASS
MISSISSIPPI • TURKEYS
VIRGINIA • STRIPERS

"The line tightened, I set the hook and the whole fish came to the surface."

The author tells the story of Howard Collins's new world-record brown. It weighted 40 pounds 4 ounces.

From "Brown Trout: A New World Record," by Michael Pearce

The Smoking Gun Photo —

This photo, along with a few others, is shown as evidence that Art Lawton's world-record muskie was falsified.

From "World-Record Muskie: Was It a Hoax?" by John Dettloff

OutdoorLife
SPECIAL

LATE-SEASON DEER
TOUGH CHALLENGES FOR HUNTERS WHO WON'T QUIT

WHY ICEFISHING TACTICS ARE DEADLY WHEN THERE'S NO ICE

SHOW-BIZ SHOOTERS: A STRONG VOICE FOR GUN OWNERS

WEST
CALIFORNIA • TROUT
OREGON • STEELHEAD
ARIZONA • BASS
WASHINGTON • CHUKAR
NEW MEXICO • RABBITS
WYOMING • SNOWSHOES

Shark Fins —

"The practice of cutting off a shark's fins and releasing the shark to swim, rudderless, to its death allows market hunters to fill their boats with fins without taking on the additional burden of a shark's total weight and volume. The gruesome technique is driven by a seemingly insatiable appetite for shark-fin soup in the Orient, where a single bowl goes for $50."

From "Predators in Peril," by Peter Goadby and George Bell

MIDWEST: EXCLUSIVE PHOTOS OF YOUR AREA'S MONSTER BUCKS

OUTDOOR LIFE
MIDWEST EDITION
A TIMES MIRROR MAGAZINE

AUGUST 1993 $2.50 CANADA $2.75

Topwater Teasers For Late-Summer
Bass Action

GPS: SPACE AGE TRAILBLAZERS TO THE RESCUE

STALK THE TALLGRASS FOR MONSTER BUCKS

COST-BUSTER CAMPING TIPS

EASY PROJECTS
■ BUILD A GUNNING DORY
■ MOUNT A SCOPE
YOU CAN DO IT!

EAST: FALL ADVENTURES—SALMON, GROUSE AND WOODCOCK

OUTDOOR LIFE
A TIMES MIRROR MAGAZINE

Bear Power!
True tales of close calls

FIRST TEST DODGE RAM: V10 POWER IN A BRAWNY NEW BODY

12-GAUGE "LITE" MORE BIRDS ... LESS KICK

CALLING HANDBOOK: TURKEYS, ELK, WHITETAILS

INTRODUCING
PRIVATE LESSONS: STEP-BY-STEP INSTRUCTIONS FOR ALL OUTDOORSMEN

OCTOBER 1993
EAST EDITION
$2.50
CANADA $2.75

New Conservation Pledge —

"It was written by Thomas Taylor of Fort Wayne, Indiana. Mr. Taylor, a policeman for 14 years in Fort Wayne, is an avid bowhunter and bass fishermen. He is a waterfowl hunter and a member of Ducks Unlimited."

From "Editorial Trails: Our New Conservation Pledge," by Vin T. Sparano

CONSERVATION PLEDGE
I PLEDGE TO PROTECT AND CONSERVE THE NATURAL RESOURCES OF AMERICA. I PROMISE TO EDUCATE FUTURE GENERATIONS SO THEY MAY BECOME CARETAKERS OF OUR WATER, AIR, LAND AND WILDLIFE.
OUTDOOR LIFE

"Arizona's Proposition 200 pitted animal rights advocates against the country's sportsmen. The way the good guys won is a lesson to all."

From "How the West Was Won," by Rick Story

"Though some states offer special opportunities to sportsmen with disabilities, many individuals simply want equal treatment."

From "Outdoors Unlimited," by Tom Huggler

SPECIAL ADVENTURE ISSUE

OUTDOORLIFE
A TIMES MIRROR MAGAZINE

DANGER IN THE WILD
BEARS ... BOARS ... BIG CATS

THE TRAIT
SURVIVORS
SHARE... DO
YOU HAVE IT?

ACCURIZING:
CUSTOM
PERFORMANCE
FROM A
STOCK RIFLE

JANUARY 1994
EAST EDITION
$2.50
CANADA $2.75

EAST
OPEN-WATER
ROUNDUP
PLUS SNAGGING
CONTROVERSY

EST: WHERE MONSTER MUSKIES LURK, RINGNECK ROUNDUP

OUTDOORLIFE

CHEL AND ZUMBO
HEIR FAVORITE
RIFLES

VEHICLES:
S NEW FOR
ORSMEN IN '95
S ... VANS ... 4x4s

now When
o Hunt Deer!
SIVE MOON TABLES
OU
BEST DAYS
BEST TIMES

ONE-MAN BOATS
COME OF AGE

HUNTING:
HOW DOGS
HELP YOU GET
FALL TURKEYS

ADVENTURE:
LIFELONG
QUEST FOR ELK

$2.50
OCTOBER 1994
MIDWEST EDITION
CANADA $2.75
A TIMES MIRROR MAGAZINE

1994

"Hard-working farmland furnishes food for our table, but it makes poor habitat for wildlife."

From "Sighting in CRP – Preserving the National Habitat," by the editors of Outdoor Life

Surviving Alone —

"Without warning, you are dropped into wilderness disaster. You could be lost, injured, caught in a storm, threatened with hypothermia or whatever your worst nightmare might be. Think quickly, what is the key to your survival?"

From "The Survivor Trait," by Larry Mueller

New Record Whitetail —

"I picked him up in my scope and fired and saw him go down when the .308 bullet hit him." On November 23, 1993, Saskatchewan hunter Milo Hanson took the greatest world record of them all, a whitetail buck scoring 213⅝ Boone and Crockett points.

From "The New World Record," by Milo Hanson as told to Jim Zumbo

Environmental Catastrophe —

This article covers the proposed New World Mine, which would threaten Yellowstone National Park.

From "Paradise Plundered," by Robert H. Boyle

SPECIAL REPORT: CONSERVING OCEAN PLANET

OUTDOOR LIFE
THE SPORTSMAN'S AUTHORITY

MARCH 1995

Turkey Hunting

HOW-TO GOBBLER HANDBOOK:
- **FOOLPROOF SETUPS**
- **CALLS THAT WORK**
- **SCOUTING BIG BIRD**
- **PATTERNING SHOTGUNS**

FISHING:
FLYFISHING FOR CARP!
... YOU CAN'T MAKE
UP THIS STUFF

BOATS:
3 FISHING BOAT BARGAINS

BONUS
THE BEST NEW FISHING TACKLE FOR 1995

VEHICLES:
FORD BRONCO VS.
CHEVY TAHOE

SHOOTING:
CARMICHEL LOOKS
AT LONG-BARREL
SHOTGUNS THAT
WILL SHOCK
TURKEY HUNTERS

$2.50
SOUTH EDITION
CANADA $2.75
A TIMES MIRROR MAGAZINE

MIDWEST: CASH IN ON SPRINGTIME POND AND PANFISHING

OUTDOOR LIFE
THE SPORTSMAN'S AUTHORITY

MAY 1995

Catch Big Walleyes!

BONUS SECTION:
PAGES PACKED WITH
DEADLY TRICKS,
LURES AND TACTICS

WE TEACH
YOU TO BE A
BASS PRO

JIM CARMICHEL
PICKS THE TOP
NEW GUNS FOR '95

WHY CRAPPIES ARE BETTER IN BED

GET A GOBBLER AT HIGH NOON

CAMPS THAT TOUGHEN UP KIDS

HUNTER ETHICS: STALKING TURKEYS

**PRIVATE LESSONS:
EXPERT ANSWERS TO
YOUR QUESTIONS**

$2.50
MIDWEST EDITION
CANADA $2.75
A TIMES MIRROR MAGAZINE

1995 Miss Kansas-USA —

"Beautiful . . . the setting, the dogs, the bird . . . but they paled in comparison with the proud hunter, Deborah Daulton, beaming from beneath her orange stocking cap . . ."

From "Miss Wingshot 1995," by the editors of Outdoor Life

1994

HAPPY HOLIDAYS

Aicha, Val, Ramona
4×5   5pt.   6pt.

"The Hull girls went three-for-three for elk last season: (from left) Aicha, 17; Valerie, 14; and Ramona, 12."

From "The Elk Girls," by the editors of Outdoor Life

BEST EASTERN BACKCOUNTRY FISHING

JULY 1996

OUTDOORLIFE
THE SPORTSMAN'S AUTHORITY SINCE 1898

ALASKA

The Great Land

20 DREAM TRIPS YOU THOUGHT YOU COULDN'T AFFORD

$2.95
CANADA $3.50
A TIMES MIRROR MAGAZINE

Vin T. Sparano —

"I planned to write my last Editorial Trails at home, but now the woods seem like a better place to talk to you."

From "A Turn in the Trail," by Vin T. Sparano, Editor

DEER OF THE YEAR CONTEST: PAGE 16

DECEMBER 1996

OUTDOORLIFE
THE SPORTSMAN'S AUTHORITY SINCE 1898

Predator Alert!

WINTER DEER TACTICS
LOWDOWN ON THE LATE RUT

REVEALED
THE SMALLMOUTH RECORD HOAX

$2.95
CANADA $3.50
A TIMES MIRROR MAGAZINE

"Hunter shoots his 8-pointer at 99."

Vern McConnell and grandson Skip Speirs admire Vern's buck. Born in 1896, Vern is the oldest Michigan hunter on record to take a deer.

From "Aged Record," by Eric Sharp

"Jim Zumbo with his colossal Montana bighorn. The 17-inch bases on the animal's horns and their sheer mass easily put this ram in the record book."

From "The Big Sheep," by Jim Zumbo

1997

"J.B. Ricks, 17, of Traverse City, poses with his first deer . . ."

Readers of *Outdoor Life* send in their photos and stories of the previous year's deer season.

From "Deer of the Year '96," by the editors of Outdoor Life

50-Inch Muskie —

"Practicing catch-and-release is the key to maintaining muskie fisheries. That's why 14-year-old J.D. Funk (above) put back this fish of a lifetime.

From "Testing the Waters: Muskellunge," by Dan Armitage

"It's already time for hunters to gear up for 1998 ballot battles in the West."

The author asks hunters, especially those in California and Utah, to get involved with their state sportsmen's groups to beat back anti-hunting challenges at the ballet box.

From "Taking the Initiatives," by Brian McCombie

1998

"*Micheal Pearce with his 10-year-old son, Jerrod. The time they've spent hunting together has strengthened their relationship.*"

From "Life Lessons," by Michael Pearce

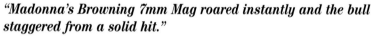

Predators —

"Hunting with a bow means you've got to get up close and personal, which requires high-tech camouflage and a knack with the coaxer call."

From "The Howl of Winter," by Gary Clancy

"Madonna's Browning 7mm Mag roared instantly and the bull staggered from a solid hit."

The author's wife, Madonna, draws a precious late-season elk tag for their home state of Wyoming. Hunting in bitterly cold temperatures, she takes a massive five-pointer.

From "Bulls Below Zero," by Jim Zumbo

"*Deep snow. Bitter cold. Tons of flushes. You just can't beat the late season.*"

From "Last Call for Grouse," by Tim Leary

THE CENTENNIAL ISSUES

"Perhaps in an era in which a person can pledge a billion dollars to charity or make $80 million tossing a ball through an iron hoop, the idea of celebrating a mere 100—of anything—is trivial. Even 100 years of existence seems almost commonplace, as Willard Scott testifies to every weekday morning.

But is '100' so easily dismissed?

General Motors hasn't yet reached that milestone. Nor has Wheaties. Or even the IRS. When you come to think about it, then, a centennial is not so much a celebration of longevity as it is of surviving change."

—Executive Editor Bob Brown's introduction to Outdoor Life's *first centennial special section, December/January 1998*

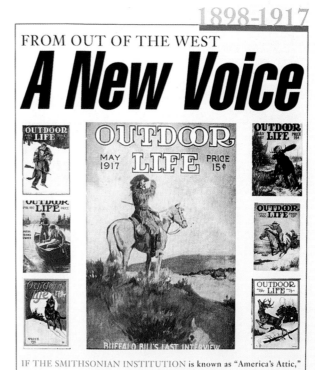

FROM OUT OF THE WEST

A New Voice

1898-1917

IF THE SMITHSONIAN INSTITUTION is known as "America's Attic," then OUTDOOR LIFE is the "Nation's Den"—crammed with 100 years of writings, illustrations, photos and advertisements created for an audience of dedicated sportsmen. To begin our centennial year, we review the highlights—and some toe-stubbings—from OUTDOOR LIFE's first two decades.

What makes *Outdoor Life* unique is that it has not merely survived change and chronicled change, it has *created* change. Beginning with the very first issue, it is clear that editor J.A. McGuire's intent was not merely to entertain and instruct sportsmen but also to serve their interests on a variety of levels.

To celebrate our 100th anniversary, each issue in 1998 contains a special eight-page centennial section highlighting a different decade in *Outdoor Life's* colorful history. They offer a glimpse at some of the best stories we've ever published along with time lines showing the evolution of hunting, fishing, game conservation, legislation and outdoor products. We also profile some of the magazine's best-known personalities, such as Zane Grey, Teddy Roosevelt, Buffalo Bill Cody and Aldo Leopold.

Our summer issue is devoted solely to our 100-year anniversary. It contains excerpts from classic *Outdoor Life* stories along with some surprises like Amelia Earhart's first flyfishing story and a day fishing for marlin with Ernest Hemingway. Other authors of note include Townsend Whelen, Russell Annabel, Joe Brooks and Jack O'Connor, as well as Charles Elliott, Jim Carmichel, Pat McManus, Jim Zumbo and Jerry Gibbs.

We also look at some of the interesting themes that have run through the magazine since its inception: adventure stories, the best of "This Happened to Me," classic bear stories, hunting and firearms, fishing and conservation—all infused with insights from the many staff members both present and past who have helped build the legacy that is *Outdoor Life.*

Todd W. Smith,
Editor-in-Chief

"This magazine celebrates its 100th birthday in 1998, which puts it among a literal handful of publications that can make that claim."
From "In the Hands of Our Friends," by Bob Brown

Old and New —

"Today's offices (below) in New York City (with, clockwise from top left, Phil Monahan, Camille Cozzone, Frank Rothmann and myself) are a far cry from the original *Outdoor Life* type room in Denver (left)."

From "Editor's Journal: On Turning 100," by Todd W. Smith

100 Years in Pictures Essayist:
Charles Elliott

By Vin T. Sparano

In 1950, nearly 50 years ago, *Outdoor Life* hired a man named Charles Newton Elliott as a Field Editor. Charlie is now 91 years old and is still on the masthead of the magazine as an active Field Editor. No other *Outdoor Life* editor can match Elliott's tenure or his influence on millions of sportsmen in America.

What do I remember most about Charlie? I remember the ultimate Southern gentleman who drove all over Covington, Georgia, on a Sunday morning to find grits for a Yankee who loves grits. Charlie hates grits and the Yankee was me!

I remember the sign above the door of a small building at the rear of Charlie's beautiful home in Georgia that read "The Pout House." Charlie explained that the Pout House is his special place he goes to when things go wrong or when he needs a quiet place to sort out his thoughts. It's also where his wife sends him when he's cranky! What's in Charlie's Pout House? Nothing special. An old mounted deer head, some turkey feathers, a manual typewriter, old fishing tackle and a few favorite books. Charlie says the world would be a better place if we all had a Pout House. He's right.

I remember when Charlie called in a big Louisiana gobbler for me when he was 87 years old. I sat motionless and frustrated, believing Charlie wasn't calling enough, when the gobbler suddenly showed up in my sights. When I asked Charlie why he didn't call more often, his reply was simple: "Son, you gotta play hard to get." The Old Professor could truly talk a turkey out of its feathers. His book, *Turkey Hunting With Charlie Elliott*, has become a classic.

12-pound Bass —

In this article, Charlie describes fishing for trophy largemouth bass on Lake Jackson in northern Florida. After a few days of tough fishing due to a recent cold front, he goes out on the lake with an old hunting and fishing partner, Ben Waddill. Ben, who's acting as guide on this trip, points to a spot in the vegetation that he wants Charlie to cast toward. Charlie writes, "I hit the bull's-eye, and let the spoon sink a couple of feet. Then I worked it away from the grass, over the top of a pad, and gently off the side toward the boat. The swirl under my lure was big enough for a 10-foot alligator."
From "Crazy with Big Bass," April 1968

"I proudly display my first Rio Grande gobbler."

Charlie accepts an invitation to hunt wild turkeys from Glenn Titus, outdoor editor of Oklahoma City's *Daily Oklahoman and Times*. After several mornings of windy weather and few chances at gobblers, Charlie spends an afternoon sitting in a heavily timbered swamp along a small stream. Although the wind is still blowing strong, Charlie goes through the ritual of yelping with his box call. His efforts are rewarded when an 18-pound gobbler comes on a beeline for the blind.
From "The Gullible Gobbler," March 1969

Charlie has written more than 20 books, including a conservation textbook that has been adopted by 40 states as their official textbook. As an *Outdoor Life* Field Editor, he continues to entertain generations of readers with tales of his hunting and fishing adventures, but his life's goal was always to teach and instill a conservation ethic in young sportsmen.

In 1995, the State of Georgia, where Elliott was the first director of the Game and Fish Commission, dedicated a 6,400-acre tract of land in Charlie's honor. Named the Charlie Elliott Wildlife Center, the land is a multi-use area that serves as a wildlife and natural resource training center for youths and adults. The area also provides hunting and fishing opportunities on 28 lakes. The Charlie Elliott Wildlife Center is an inspiring tribute to a man who has devoted a lifetime to conservation and education.

In 1997, in a continuing tribute, Georgia dedicated The Charlie Elliott Visitors' Center at the Charlie Elliott Wildlife Center. More than 40,000 students a year will use the Center. The facility will also house an Outdoor Learning Center to teach educators how to use the outdoors as a classroom.

One of the unique features of the Visitor's Center will be the recreation of Charlie's den, where he has spent a lifetime writing for *Outdoor Life*. Visitors will be able to see the Dall ram over his fireplace, the bear and wolf rugs on the floor, the huge mule deer over his old desk and typewriter and all the memorabilia of a lifetime of outdoor adventures.

Charlie and I have been good friends for nearly 40 years and I would like to share a couple of quotes that will tell you more about this man than I can.

"If you use your eyes, ears and a little bug juice, a most delightful period that anyone can spend is sitting quietly in the woods."

"When I go, I want to ask Polly to open the doors of my den and ask my friends to drink all my bourbon."

Those of us who have shared time and words with Charlie Elliott are indeed privileged.

—Vin T. Sparano,
Editor Emeritus/Senior Field Editor

". . . if I covered no more than 100 yards of stream and didn't see a rainbow or a brookie, this was going to be a perfect day."

Charlie returns to the upper Bald River in eastern Tennessee for a slow-paced, peaceful day of trout fishing. While sitting on a streamside boulder, he flips a Royal Coachman out on top of the current just to test whether he'd be able to follow it with his aging eyes. He writes, "The fly didn't float down gently, but plopped rather awkwardly at the edge of the current. If lightning had struck the rock on which I sat, I would have been no more surprised than I was at the wash of color and the bucking fly rod in my hand . . . It was by far the largest rainbow I had ever seen on this stretch of upper river."
From "My Return to Bald River," February 1990

The Autobiographer —
"Any man must certainly have grown into an age of absurdity when, in his late eighties, the urge overpowers him to forego his afternoon nap and instead, sit down to begin a book."
From An Outdoor Life: The Autobiography of Charlie Elliott, *p. vii*